Divine Names

Harness the Power of Allah's 99 Names
for Success in Work and Life

SARAH GULFRAZ

Copyright © 2025 Sarah Gulfraz

Sarah Gulfraz has asserted her right to be identified as the author of this Work in accordance with the Copyright, Designs and Patents Act 1988.

All rights reserved.

No portion of this book may be reproduced in any form, stored in a retrieval system, stored in a database, or published/transmitted in any form or by any means, electronic, mechanical, photocopying, recording or otherwise, without prior written permission of the publisher.

Dedication

~ **Bismillah** ~

May Allah (swt) accept our efforts and grant us success in this life and the next. Ameen.

In dedication to my loving family and all their support.

Contents

1. Introduction — 1
2. Introduction to the 99 Names of Allah (SWT) — 4
3. Using the Names of Allah for Personal Development — 13
4. Using the Names of Allah for Professional Development — 31
5. Strengthening Relationships Using the Names of Allah — 42
6. Overcoming Challenges and Stress with Divine Names — 57
7. Enhancing Spiritual Connection through the Names of Allah — 69
8. Utilising the Names of Allah (SWT) for Personal and Professional Goals — 83
9. Teaching and Sharing the Names of Allah (SWT) with Others — 97
10. Reflecting on the Impact of Using Divine Names — 104
11. Continuing Your Journey with the Names of Allah (SWT) — 113
12. Conclusion — 118

Find Out More — 120

Chapter One

Introduction

One of the most basic human wants is to have a purpose in life. The majority of people, however, struggle to identify their life's purpose, and it's true that modern living tends to divert people from their actual objectives. It often forces us to confront who we are, what we truly value, and where we go from here with the challenges and opportunities life feeds us. For centuries, cultures and beliefs have pondered these questions, but for many, the answers remain elusive.

This continuous process of development and self-discovery demonstrates how our vision and knowledge are constantly changing. However, for the seekers of meaning and purpose in life, there is a unique and profound journey that takes place via the 99 beautiful names of Allah (SWT), a path which can change a person's personal and professional life.

Knowing Allah (SWT) through His lovely names is possibly the most profound of all the paths we can take to understand love in its purest form. These 99 names, which have their roots in Islamic tradition and the Quran, provide insight into the limitless nature of Allah (SWT).

Asma ul Husna, Allah's (SWT) 99 names, are a mosaic of His countless qualities, each of which reflects a distinct aspect of the Creator that speaks to the human condition. These names describe Allah's (SWT) activities in the world and His relationship with creation; they are more than merely labels. These names are how Allah (SWT) presents Himself in the Quran, establishing a basis for compassion and love.

> *Allah (SWT) says in the Quran: "He is Allah: the Creator, the Inventor, the Shaper. He alone has the Most Beautiful Names. Whatever is in the heavens and the earth constantly glorifies Him. And He is the Almighty, All-Wise". (Quran 59:24)*

This book explores how the 99 names can be a powerful resource for anyone seeking to grow and succeed in various areas of life.

The significance and intent of each name, as well as the ways in which these divine names can alter behaviour, attitude, and mental processes in response to both personal and professional obstacles, every name has a lesson that, if learnt, will enable us to cultivate the traits that allow us to advance higher, whether it's the fortitude we acquire in the face of hardship or the compassion we show in our relationships. Asma ul Husna serves as a spiritual mentor, helping us reach our goals – be it career success, improved relationships, or self-peace.

You cannot really enjoy life if you're not supported by a greater power or force. As the saying goes, "the spiritual governs the physical." A higher power oversees everything in this world, and by aligning yourself with the "right" higher power, you can transform the course of your life. To receive divine blessings, you must establish a solid relationship with it.

Using the Divine Names as instruments for personal development is among the most significant ways to interact with the highest power, Allah Almighty (SWT). Every name gives us a chance to discover who we are on the inside and awakens our spiritual potential to strive to improve ourselves and the lives of people around us. Through reflection and practice, these divine names can help us grow emotionally, mentally, and spiritually.

Divine guidance is not only limited to our personal growth but influences our professional lives in profound ways. For instance, taking help from these divine names in a professional context entails making an effort to maintain integrity, openness, and accountability, all of which eventually promote respect and trust among partners, clients, and coworkers. When we remain mindful of these holy attributes, we create a boundary around ourselves that helps us act in alignment with values that promote a positive and productive environment.

By discovering the "divine within," we give ourselves access to a reservoir of knowledge, fortitude, and meaning that can help us overcome obstacles in life and lead more genuine lives. This book examines the meaning of connecting with the divine inside, useful techniques for calling forth this force through holy names, and the life-changing effects it can have.

This book is an open invitation for you to engage in a journey of spiritual and personal transformation. Exploring the 99 beautiful names of Allah (SWT) opens up whole new ideas and inspiration that touch every part of our lives. Every name is a special key to comprehending the attributes of Allah (SWT), which also helps us comprehend our own. Over time, more reflection and implementation will show that those divine qualities also manifest us in a life where we serve ourselves with purpose, fulfilment and success. As you use the power of Allah's (SWT) names to effect positive change and succeed in your personal and professional endeavours, let this book serve as a guide.

Let's dive in!

Chapter Two

Introduction to the 99 Names of Allah (SWT)

Significance and Meaning

The names of Allah (SWT) are revered in Islam and are referred to as Asma ul Husna (The Most Beautiful Names). Each of these 99 names gives us a different perspective on Allah's (SWT) nature, might, and kindness. Muslims think that by knowing, comprehending, and addressing Allah (SWT) by these names, they might deepen their relationship with Him, strengthen their faith, and lead better lives.

Knowing Allah (SWT) through His lovely names is possibly the most profound of all the paths we can take to understand love in its purest form. This journey, which has its roots in Islamic tradition and the Quran, invites us to develop a loving, intimate, and conscious relationship with our Creator by providing a glimpse into the limitless nature of Allah (SWT).

Understanding the Concept of Asma ul Husna (The Beautiful Names of Allah)

The Quran and Hadith reveal Allah's (SWT) 99 names, each representing His attributes and characteristics. Some reflect His strength, while others embody His charity. We can strengthen our relationship with Allah (SWT) by being aware of these names, each a key to understanding a distinct facet of His character. These names are more than merely labels; they describe Allah's (SWT) attributes in the world and His relationship with creation. Through them, Allah (SWT) presents Himself in the Quran, establishing a basis for compassion and love.

In addition to memorising these names, we are urged to consider their meanings and use them in our day-to-day activities. We can live a life more in accordance with Islamic principles and become closer to Allah (SWT) by doing this.

> *Prophet Muhammad (PBUH) said: "Indeed, Allah has ninety-nine names. Whoever memorises them will enter Paradise." (Sahih Muslim)*

The universe as a whole was created by the Almighty Allah. He possesses every virtue, known or unknown, imaginable or unimaginable. His absolute being is reflected in this planet. He alone possesses all the glory, splendours, and majesty since He is the Creator. Asma ul Husna outlines His qualities and characteristics. Learning about Allah (SWT) is the same as learning about Asma ul Husna.

A person is fulfilling his purpose when he engages in learning about Allah Almighty (SWT); if he disregards the issue, he is failing to fulfil his purpose.

Although memorising Allah's (SWT) names is not mandatory, doing so has the serious benefit of making your duas consistently brimming with love for your Creator, as each emotion, need, and situation has a name. Every name demonstrates a quality that gives us comfort and fortitude, particularly in times of adversity. Knowing Allah's (SWT) names turns into a personal act of devotion that encourages us to contemplate, comprehend, and absorb the essence of Allah (SWT).

The Spiritual and Practical Significance of Each Name

Let's have a look at the 99 Names of Allah (Asma ul-Husna), along with their meanings and some of the benefits associated with each name:

Historical and Theological Context

The Origins and Importance of the 99 Names in Islamic Tradition

The Islamic belief is that Allah (SWT) revealed Himself to the Prophet Muhammad (PBUH) through His traits or qualities. The 99 Names, which include The All-Merciful, The Healer, and The Light, each stand for a distinct character or attribute of Allah (SWT). Scholars first documented the 99 Names and used them to make supplications during their prayers many centuries ago. Over time, these prayers have been included in Islamic customs and are frequently offered as a way to meditate and establish a connection with Allah (SWT).

A significant component of Islamic mysticism and theology is the 99 Names of Allah (SWT). Reciting the 99 names, according to several Muslim scholars, can promote spiritual fulfilment and tranquillity while strengthening the bond between Muslims and their creator. In other theological traditions and civilisations, the 99 Names of Allah (SWT) are likewise a hot topic. Although the meaning and origin of these names haven't changed, there has been significant discussion about how best to translate them into English or other languages besides Arabic.

This is because certain translations might not convey each name's actual meaning correctly. For example, many Muslims believe that "Allah" means "the One True Allah (SWT)," while a popular translation implies that it means "Allah (SWT)." Therefore, it's crucial for Muslims to study the different translations of the 99 Names to better comprehend their meanings.

Throughout history, the 99 Names of Allah (SWT) have been utilised as a form of meditation and devotion, constituting a significant aspect of Islamic tradition and culture. To promote serenity and spiritual fulfilment, they are frequently chanted during prayers or utilised during periods of reflection in modern times. One can cultivate a deeper connection with Allah (SWT) and learn more about the lovely facets of Islam by learning more about these names and their origins, meanings, and significance to Islam.

One can have a deeper understanding of Islam's teachings and strengthen their relationship with Allah (SWT) by learning more about their history, significance, and meanings. With this knowledge, the beauty of Islam in all its manifestations can be better appreciated. For many generations to come, the 99 Names of Allah (SWT) will continue to play a significant role in contemporary Muslim life worldwide.

How are the 99 Names used in the Quran and Hadith?

In the Quran, Allah's (SWT) names are used interchangeably to highlight certain attributes of Allah (SWT), be they of mercy, power, wisdom, or justice. Each name denotes some special way that Allah (SWT) interacts with His creation.

The Quran and Hadith speak directly about Allah (SWT) and describe His qualities, names, and deeds, guiding us to know Him more deeply. The Quran, as the ultimate and unaltered words of Allah (SWT), leaves no place for doubt or confusion in understanding Him. Similarly, the words of His Messenger (PBUH) are a true reflection of Allah's (SWT) message. Hence, they form a reliable path for gaining knowledge about Allah (SWT).

> *Allah (SWT) says: "And if anyone of the Mushrikoon [polytheists idolaters pagans disbelievers in the Oneness of Allah] seeks your protection then grant him protection so that he may hear the Word of Allah [the Quran] ...)"* (Quran 9:6)

> *"Those who remained behind will say when you set out toward the war booty to take it, 'Let us follow you.' They wish to change the Words of Allah." (Quran 48:15)*

These two passages demonstrate that Allah the Almighty's (SWT) words and speech, as revealed to His Prophet Muhammad (PBUH), are contained in the Quran. According to Jabir ibn Abdullah (RA), during the Haj season, the Prophet (PBUH) would extend invitations to Muslims and would say:

> *"Who are willing to give me asylum so that I can convey the Speech of my Lord, for the Quraysh have prevented me from conveying the Speech of my Lord" (Tirmidhi and Ahmad)*

Applying the Names in Daily Life

It is useless to just commit a number of words to memory if they don't actually affect our lives. So it's really essential to examine all of Allah's (SWT) lovely names and how they affect us if we want to truly understand what they imply.

Overview of How These Names Can Be Integrated into Various Aspects of Life

A Muslim's faith is strengthened when they are aware of Allah's (SWT) names. Knowing that Allah (SWT) is Al-Khaliq (The Creator) of everything serves as a reminder of both His omnipotence and the reason we are here. Our faith in Allah (SWT) is strengthened, particularly in difficult circumstances, when we consider that He is Ar-Razzaq (The Provider), the source of all our bounties. Even though life might be difficult, the names of Allah (SWT) can provide solace. For instance, recalling that Allah (SWT) is Al-Hadi (The Guide) can give hope to someone feeling lost.

Thinking of Allah (SWT) as Al-Ghaffar (The Forgiver) can help someone battling guilt. Based on the circumstance, each name provides a distinct kind of consolation and security. Muslims are also guided in their daily lives by the 99 Names of Allah (SWT).

For example, understanding that Allah (SWT) is As-Sabur (The Patient) inspires us to be patient in trying circumstances, while understanding that Allah (SWT) is Al-Adl (The Just) teaches us to treat others fairly. We can live better, more moral lives thanks to the practical implications of Allah's (SWT) names, which go beyond mere theory. Allah's (SWT) immense kindness and compassion are among the most important lessons to be learnt from Asma ul Husna, the 99 Names of Allah (SWT).

Numerous titles, such as Ar-Rahman (The Most Merciful) and Al-Wadud (The Loving), serve as a constant reminder to Muslims of Allah's (SWT) kindness and love. These names remind us that Allah (SWT) is always willing to pardon us and guide us back to the correct path, regardless of how many mistakes we make.

Muslims often use Allah's (SWT) names to convey their emotions during prayer. For example, someone seeking forgiveness might address Allah (SWT) as Al-Ghafoor (The Most Forgiving). Or someone praying for healing might invoke Him as Ash-Shafi (The Healer). By using these names, Muslims experience a closer relationship with their Creator. Allah's (SWT) 99 names are not merely for education or memorisation but mean much more.

The 99 Names of Allah (SWT) are meant to inspire Muslims to embody these virtues. For instance, since Allah (SWT) is Al-Adl (The Just), we should strive to treat others with fairness and justice. Similarly, recognising Allah (SWT) as As-Sabur (The Patient) encourages us to be patient. We grow as individuals and become closer to Allah (SWT). Including these in our duas, or daily prayers, deepens our connection with Him.

You might invoke Allah (SWT) As-Salam (The Source of tranquilly) to seek Him for tranquilly if you're feeling nervous. You can invoke Allah (SWT) as Al-Fattah (The Opener) if you want to succeed. Using these names will allow you to have more intimate conversations with Allah (SWT). Acquiring knowledge of Allah's (SWT) 99 names has the potential to transform your life.

Yes, it can feel overwhelming to learn them all, but to begin with, learn a few names at a time. Consider the significance of each name and how it relates to your life. For instance, knowing about Al-Latif (The Subtle, The Kind) might serve as a helpful reminder that Allah's (SWT) generosity is present in even the smallest, most imperceptible ways while you're going through a difficult time.

Setting Intentions for Using the Names in Personal and Professional Settings

We can all set up a decent routine and concentrate on our objectives, striving for steady and intentional growth every day. With determination and patience, we maximise the advantages and rewards of our efforts. However, nothing can be accomplished without Allah's (SWT) will and assistance; seeking His help should be the primary goal of whatever we do.

Applying the beautiful names of Allah (SWT) as guiding principles in our personal and professional lives requires pure intention. This practice is important as the Quran repeatedly reminds us of its power and significance with reverence.

> *"And Allah's names are the best names, so call on Him and leave those who violate the sanctity of His Names. They shall be recompensed for what they did." (Quran 7:180)*

By learning Allah's (SWT) names, you can stay connected to His presence throughout the day, helping you navigate deadlines and the everyday responsibilities of contemporary life. Remembering His names reminds you that He is a guiding light, all-knowing, kind, benevolent, and the Creator of all.

Practical Tips to Memorise

To successfully and meaningfully memorise the 99 Names of Allah (SWT), the following will help:

The first step is to get a deeper grasp of their significance. Utilise mnemonic devices and group names to help you organise your memorisation process. Use association and visualisation strategies to develop rhymes or mental pictures for every name.

Before trying to memorise each name by heart, you must first comprehend the true meaning and significance of each name. Understanding the characteristics and attributes that each name represents is necessary for memorisation. Consider the name Ar-Rahman, which translates to "The Most Gracious." Consider for a moment how incredibly compassionate and lovely this name is. Understand its impact on your life and relationship with Allah (SWT).

As soon as you wake up and before bed or after Maghrib, recite the names you've memorised. It only takes two minutes to recite all of the names at once. We can certainly devote this much time to memorisation, which carries such honour and reward, can't we? Simply recite them while following the list in Arabic. Choose a time that works for you and stick to it.

Learning the 99 Names of Allah (SWT) is a life-changing and spiritually fulfilling endeavour. We understand that this journey is more than just a recitation exercise; it's a deep relationship with the Divine. May every recitation be a sincere invocation that broadens your comprehension of Allah's (SWT) qualities and cultivates a relationship that goes beyond simple word memorisation. Sincerity and devotion transform this journey into a bright route to a deeper spiritual life.

Chapter Three

Using the Names of Allah for Personal Development

Fostering Self-Improvement with Allah's Attributes

The idea of personal development in Islam is firmly based on the knowledge that serving and worshipping Allah (SWT) is our ultimate goal in life. This encompasses how we behave in all facets of our lives and goes beyond the conventional ideas of worshipping at a mosque or just praying.

> *"And I did not create the jinn and mankind except to worship me." (Quran 51:56)*

Accordingly, from an Islamic standpoint, personal development entails more than merely attaining financial success or personal fulfilment. To help humanity and fulfil our obligation to Allah (SWT), we must strive to become the best versions of ourselves.

Let's now consider what self-improvement means from an Islamic standpoint and why it's even necessary. It refers to the deliberate act of bettering oneself by improving one's abilities, skills, well-being, emotional health, habits, and the methods for continuous growth in these areas.

Personal development is an ongoing activity, so it's not just something you learn and then stop; it's thinking about things you should be learning and growing on all the time. According to this theory, you should have the willpower and the belief that you can improve yourself in a variety of ways.

> *"Truly I was sent as a Prophet for the purpose of perfecting human character." (Al-Muwatta)*

This hadith explains a crucial tenet of Islam: the purifying of one's own character to develop oneself. Muslims who practise Islam are taught to follow the teachings of Prophet Muhammad (PBUH) and the Quran to improve themselves.

A Muslim who is committed to improving himself or herself in all facets of life will exude excellent character to others, which will benefit society as a whole.

> *"All actions are judged by their intentions, and each person will be rewarded according to his or her intention." (Sahih Bukhari)*

This dynamic shift starts at the individual level with the definition and purification of one's intention or niyyah. Seeking Allah's (PBUH) pleasure is the right aim and objective to have on the path to self-purification.

Before trying to influence others, one must first concentrate on bettering themselves. Muslims must strive for a pure intention throughout their self-improvement path before attempting to achieve spiritual purification through Tazkiya or the cleansing of the heart.

> *"Truly Allah (SWT) does not change the condition of a people until they change what is in themselves." (Quran 13:11)*

By deepening your understanding of the five pillars of Islam and their practical application, you can concentrate on the core of Ibadah – the worship of the one and only Allah (SWT) – which serves as the foundation for self-improvement and purification. Establish a consistent prayer schedule as directed by Allah (SWT), and strive to remember Him throughout your day. This heightened awareness will make you more mindful of your actions, and you will be less likely to do something that might anger Him. Develop integrity, diligence, and moral behaviour to elevate your personal standards and character.

Moreover, developing oneself by considering the traits of Allah (SWT) inspires one to live forth virtues like justice, mercy, and patience every day. It deepens the relationship with Allah (SWT), encouraging thankfulness, modesty, and dependence on Him. Frequent prayer and recollection increase spiritual awareness, which promotes emotional fortitude and accountability. Thinking about these qualities encourages personal development and aligns actions with faith. This method fosters a well-rounded, purpose-driven life based on divine direction.

Reflecting on the Names to Build Personal Qualities

Reflecting on Asma ul Husna (The Most Beautiful Names) provides valuable insights for developing one's character. Every name displays a heavenly quality that acts as a template for character development and human behaviour. Here are some thoughts on how to develop personal traits by internalising and living up to seven of Allah's (SWT) names:

As-Sabur (The Patient) – Cultivating Patience

In the fast-paced world of today, patience is a trait that is frequently disregarded. It might be difficult to maintain composure when we're inundated with requests, expectations, and distractions.

For many of us, the smallest wait irritates us because we're so accustomed to instant gratification. Our hectic lives often leave us impatient – not only with ourselves but with one another.

A lot of us don't tolerate errors, slowness, or imperfections. We want things to be perfect, and we want results. Sometimes, we're restless even when we make dua, expecting Allah (SWT) to grant us our exact desires right away.

Allah (SWT), As-Sabur, the Most Patient, starkly contrasts the impatience that characterises humans. This lovely quality has a lot to teach us. Let's look at this quality of Allah (SWT) with careful attention.

Allah (SWT) is As-Sabur, The Most Persistent and Patient. He waits for the right moment and doesn't act rashly. Although He has the authority to punish wrongdoers, He gives us time to turn from our sins and modify our ways to return to the correct path.

Allah (SWT) continues to bestow upon us countless blessings every day in spite of our transgressions. He is always ready to pardon our sins and give us a fresh start. We should feel a huge sense of relief and comfort from this. As-Sabur delays our punishment even when we disobey Him, allowing us time to turn from our sins.

> *"Verily, the angel on the left side will raise his pen over the error or sin of a Muslim servant for six hours. If he sincerely regrets it and seeks forgiveness from Allah, the angel will throw it aside. Otherwise, he will record it as one sin." (Al-Mujam al-Kabir)*

Even when we falter, Allah (SWT) notices and values our efforts. In fact, He is immensely forgiving toward His slaves who strive to please Him, even if they stumble along the way.

Allah (SWT) does not demand perfection from us; rather, He values our perseverance and willingness to keep trying.

> *The Prophet (PBUH) said: "Allah Almighty says: Whoever comes with a good deed will have the reward of ten like it and even more. Whoever comes with an evil deed will be recompensed for one evil deed like it or he will be forgiven. Whoever draws close to me by the length of a hand, I will draw close to him by the length of an arm. Whoever draws close to me by the length of an arm, I will draw close to him by the length of a fathom. Whoever comes to me walking, I will come to him running. Whoever meets me with enough sins to fill the earth, not associating any partners with Me, I will meet him with as much forgiveness." (Sahih Muslim)*

Reflecting on our Creator's patience and mercy can bring us profound inner peace. He knows when we struggle to maintain our faith and never lets our efforts to please Him go unnoticed.

Just imagine—we only need to move in His direction, and As-Sabur will rush to us.

As Muslims, we know that patience is an essential quality deeply ingrained in our faith. Sabr refers to the ability to remain composed and serene in the face of adversity.

> *As Allah (SWT) says in the Quran: "And indeed, with hardship comes ease" (Quran 2:155)*

This verse highlights the idea that patience involves more than just enduring hardships; it entails seeking peace and ease in the midst of them.

> *The Prophet Muhammad (PBUH) also emphasised the importance of patience when he said, "Patience is half of faith." (Sahih Bukhari)*

Al-Hakim (The All-Wise) – Cultivating Wisdom

Allah (SWT) is Al-Hakim, the Wisest and Most Prudent. He is free from mistakes and misunderstandings and can distinguish between right and wrong. His creations in life and nature are precise and flawless. He alone is capable of determining the value of anything.

> *"And whosoever is granted wisdom is indeed granted abundant good." (Quran 2:269)*

Among Allah's (SWT) divine names, Al-Hakim holds a special closeness to people than others. It reminds believers of His wisdom and guidance in their lives. Likewise, the name "the Lord" is considered closest to the hearts of people. The All-Mighty Lord, Allah (SWT), responds to this by saying:

> *"So wait patiently for your Lord's Decision, for verily you are under Our Eyes; and glorify the Praises of your Lord when you get up from sleep" (Quran 52:48)*

This demonstrates unequivocally that Allah (SWT), the Lord, who is all-knowing, all-wise, and most kind, alone has the authority to decide all questions and matters.

DIVINE NAMES

The Arabic word "Hakeem" refers to someone who is highly qualified and whose work is perfect, i.e. faultless. For instance, a carpenter's job is not good enough if he doesn't cut a piece of wood precisely. In this instance, we could state: "His work would be flawless and error-free if his calculations were correct." The more precise the calculations, the better and more error-free the outcome.

While cheap machines are rife with flaws and problems, expensive devices are typically flawless. In actuality, precision and flawlessness are crucial components of high-quality machinery. They are more costly and valued because of this.

Because he's skilled at measuring, calculating, and designing, Hakeem denotes "someone who does his work most efficiently and perfectly." And because Allah (SWT) is Al-Hakim (All Wise), everything He produces has flawless, faultless measurements.

Imagine creating a galaxy, an atom, an elephant, a fly, an ant, or any other kind of creature! All of them are flawless and demonstrate Allah's (SWT) supreme divine wisdom:

> "It is He (Allah) who made everything that He has created perfect, and began the creation of man from clay." (Quran 32:7)

Consider the human body: the precise concentration of salt in the blood that flows through your veins and arteries is 0.78%. Blood corpuscles would contract and result in instant death if this precise salt content dropped. Conversely, if it rose, the cells would rupture and result in instant death. The ratio of salt in human blood has been determined by whom?

The kidneys' ability to maintain this precise amount of salt in the blood is a gift from Allah (SWT), the Most Benevolent! In addition, there are 2.5 billion different kinds of tissues worldwide. This indicates that there is just one person on the planet with a tissue type comparable to yours. Therefore, Al-Hakim, Allah (SWT), is the One who makes everything perfect.

> *As the Quran says: "He (Allah) has created everything and has measured it exactly according to its due measurements." (Quran 25:2)*

> *"It is He (Allah) Who has created seven heavens, one above another; you can see no fault in the creation of the Most Gracious. Then, look again: can you see any rifts?" (Quran 67:3)*

Since Allah (SWT) is Hakeem (All-Wise), all that occurs in the world is solely the result of His divine will; if He desires something to occur, it does. Allah's (SWT) divine will is linked to His perfect divine wisdom, which is linked to absolute goodness and guarantees that everything He wills will unavoidably come to fruition.

Only Allah's (SWT) supreme divine will and wisdom could cause a tree's leaves to fall. Too many ostensibly bad things wind up being wonderful, and there is no injustice in the truest sense of the word in Allah's (SWT) realm. As it is said, even the unjust, tyrannical rulers or leaders in this world are part of Allah's (SWT) plan.

Allah's (SWT) wisdom is evident in the balance and purpose of creation. Reflecting on Al-Hakim encourages us to seek understanding and thoughtful decision-making. This includes learning from experiences and considering the consequences of our actions. Pause before making decisions to evaluate all perspectives and align choices with a higher purpose.

Enhancing Self-Awareness and Self-Confidence

Allah (SWT) has given each human being a special talent that, when used appropriately, might help us all become better people. This gift allows us to become more compassionate, understanding, and perceptive. It doesn't grant us the power to fly or become invisible, but it's an extraordinary gift nonetheless: self-awareness.

In the Holy Quran, Allah (SWT) makes it very evident that people are the best creation. We're superior to all other creations because of the wisdom Allah (SWT), our Creator, has given us. Every human has some level of self-consciousness, and the more we hone our "awareness," the more we will be able to comprehend both ourselves and other people. However, we have great control over how we conduct our lives thanks to this "superpower."

> *Allah the Exalted says in the Holy Quran: "Surely, We have created man in the best make." (Quran 95:5)*

As Muslims, self-improvement and introspection are essential elements of our faith. Indeed, Islam stated more than 1400 years ago that the greatest jihad is the battle of self-reformation. Numerous verses in the Holy Quran likewise exhort Muslims to "ponder" and "reflect." Psychology is now beginning to recognise the advantages of self-awareness as well. Being more self-aware enables us to have spiritually satisfying lives and overcome our shortcomings.

In Islam, cultivating self-awareness and introspection is crucial for spiritual development. Self-awareness enables you to comprehend your ideas, feelings, and actions and strengthens your relationship with Allah (SWT). It also makes you more responsible to Allah (SWT), promoting a more developed spiritual path.

Introspection promotes personal growth by examining one's goals, behaviours, and beliefs in light of Islamic teachings. Embodying self-reflection can help one discover hidden strengths and shortcomings and enhance spiritual development. In Islam, this introspective and self-awareness process is a life-changing way to live a more purposeful and happy spiritual existence.

Self-awareness boosts confidence, and true self-assurance comes from recognising the positive traits Allah (SWT) has bestowed upon you and striving to cultivate those that benefit you. If you abuse or misuse it, you'll be overcome with pride and self-praise, causing you to reject the blessing Allah (SWT) has bestowed upon you.

It's crucial to look gratefully at the abilities and qualities Allah (SWT) has given you, as this mindset will foster self-confidence. Muslims who are looking for strategies to boost their confidence must refrain from using derogatory language, such as claiming a lack of confidence or believing that success in their career is unattainable. Prior setbacks and challenging situations shouldn't deter them, as dwelling on them will only undermine their efforts and lead to a negative view of their accomplishments.

We're all endowed with distinct personalities, talents, and weaknesses, as well as distinctive skill sets that we can utilise for the benefit of our families, the world, and ourselves. Knowing oneself is a lifetime task, and the more you do it consciously, the better, In sha'Allah.

Allah's (SWT) beautiful names inspire confidence and self-awareness by emulating heavenly qualities. Reflecting on names like Ash-Shakoor cultivates thankfulness, Al-Hakim promotes wisdom, and Al-Wadud motivates compassion. By internalising these traits, we can develop a purposeful existence, align our actions with divine teachings, and transform our shortcomings into strengths. Through this path of self-improvement, our relationship with Allah (SWT) is strengthened, and our faith is deepened.

Using Names That Reflect Divine Attributes to Boost Self-esteem and Confidence

In Islam, a person's relationship with Allah (SWT) is closely related to their sense of self-worth. A strong sense of self-worth is founded on the knowledge that the Creator uniquely created and treasured each person. Islam urges its adherents to acknowledge and value their intrinsic value as people.

How we feel about ourselves is influenced by our sense of self-worth. It's our self-perception and the degree to which we regard ourselves as individuals. Being happy with our Allah (SWT) given talents and skills is a sign of having a good sense of self-worth. It's crucial to have a strong feeling of self-worth. Self-confidence has an impact on everything we do and the people around us. We're more inclined to set reasonable objectives, pursue our dreams, and look out for others as well as ourselves.

A self-assured person can effectively manage themselves, navigate difficult circumstances, and overcome challenges. Self-confidence not only enables an individual to make the most of their potential and abilities, but it's also key to opening up to others and interacting effectively with them. It empowers them to succeed in the present and reach their goals for the future, bringing stability, reassurance, happiness, and the thrill of success.

Self-worth and self-esteem are increased by learning the Asma ul Husna by heart. Self-esteem grows when one realises that Allah (SWT), as Al-Khaliq (The Creator), created humans with care and purpose. Self-esteem is increased when one acknowledges that each person is unique.

One is encouraged to have confidence by the Guardian of Faith. Developing self-confidence is one of the key advantages of memorising Allah's (SWT) 99 Names. Al-Karim (the Generous) encourages self-worth and humility. Since Allah (SWT) is the source of all advantages, one should be thankful and modest about their abilities.

Recognising one's individual talents and acknowledging Allah (SWT) as Al-Musawwir (The Shaper of Beauty) boosts self-esteem, as it fosters inner serenity, stress alleviation, and the resolution of psychological disorders by establishing a strong spiritual bond and connection with the Almighty.

Moreover, memorising these names cultivates compassion and self-esteem while empowering individuals to confront life's obstacles with fortitude and perseverance.

Examples of Specific Names for Personal Empowerment

The 99 Names of Allah (SWT), or Asma ul Husna, is a powerful source of motivation for self-improvement and empowerment. Here are a few instances, along with their empowering meanings.

Al-Wahhab, also known as The Bestower, serves as a reminder of Allah's (SWT) unending generosity in bestowing benefits and gifts. When we reflect on this name, we're motivated to give in our own lives and give freely to others without anticipating anything in return. It also cultivates thankfulness by motivating us to acknowledge and value the resources and opportunities bestowed upon us.

Al-Qawiyy (The Strong) talks about unbounded power and might. Meditating on this name can strengthen our inner resilience, enabling us to face obstacles head-on with bravery and resolve. It reminds us that, particularly in trying times, we may all discover power within ourselves.

Al-Hakim (The All-Wise) emphasises the importance of wisdom in making choices. Adopting this quality promotes deliberate introspection in our decisions and behaviours. We can successfully negotiate the difficulties of life by pursuing knowledge and insight.

The virtue of patience is taught by Al-Saboor (The Most Patient). Perseverance is often necessary for life's challenges, and this name serves as a reminder that patience in the face of adversity eventually leads to progress and ease. It gives us comfort in knowing that difficulties are transitory and that help is on the way.

The quest for knowledge is encouraged by Al-Alim (The All-Knowing). Knowing that all knowledge eventually leads back to Allah's (SWT) name inspires us to pursue study and development, whether in self-awareness or comprehending the world around us.

We're reassured by Al-Razzaq (The Sustainer) that Allah (SWT) is the ultimate source of abundance and sustenance. Putting our faith in this name encourages self-assurance and diligence because we know that Allah (SWT) will provide for our needs.

Al-Mu'izz (The Honour-Giver) teaches us the importance of respecting ourselves and preserving our dignity. This name ensures that our character stays honourable and upright by encouraging us to act honourably and pursue honour through good deeds.

Al-Wadud (The Most Loving) is a manifestation of the kindness and love of Allah (SWT). Contemplating His name inspires us to cultivate positive interactions and inner tranquillity, inspiring us to show affection, generosity, and compassion to both ourselves and others.

Lastly, Al-Fattah (The Opener) give us hope, reminding us that there is always a way to overcome any challenge. By trusting in this quality, we develop endurance and hope, understanding that Allah (SWT) prepares the path for prosperity and comfort.

These names reflect the attributes of Allah (SWT) and serve as tenets for individual development. By thinking about them and adjusting our lives to reflect their deeper significance, we can discover strength in faith, patience, wisdom, and love.

Seeking Forgiveness and Self-Renewal

We should never give up or cease pleading with Allah (SWT) for pardon for our transgressions. The Prophet (PBUH) illustrates the significance of asking for forgiveness in one of his narrations:

> *"O people! Turn to Allah in repentance and seek His forgiveness, for surely I make repentance a hundred times every day." (Sahih Muslim)*

According to the Noble Prophet (PBUH), repentance is such a tremendous act of devotion that it can totally erase one's sins:

> *"One who repents from sins is like one without sin." (Sunah Ibn Majah)*

Repentance is a worshipful deed that cleanses the soul and draws the slave nearer to His Lord. It relieves guilt from the heart, strengthens a believer's faith, and prevents him from succumbing to lust and cravings. A person who honestly seeks forgiveness from Allah (SWT) after committing a sin will discover that Allah (SWT) is prepared to accept his repentance and grant him forgiveness.

> *Allah (SWT) says in the Quran: "And whoever does a wrong or wrongs himself, but then seeks forgiveness from Allah, he will find Allah forgiving and merciful." (Quran, 4:110)*

Reflect on Allah's (SWT) immense love, kindness, and compassion! As the Sovereign Lord, Allah (SWT) alone is worthy of worship, and the least He desires is that no partners or associates be ascribed to Him. Following that, Allah (SWT) pledges to pardon and show mercy to anybody who repents and expresses a true desire for forgiveness.

Shirk (polytheism), which is the affiliation of partners with Allah (SWT), is something that Allah (SWT) will never pardon. Only those who die upholding Islamic monotheism, or Tawheed, and abstaining from all forms of shirk can be forgiven. Allah (SWT), the Almighty, emphasised this in the Quran.

However, if a person seeks forgiveness from Allah (SWT), the Almighty, at the time of death, when encountering the angels, or when the sun rises from the west on the Day of Judgement, they will not be pardoned. The following statements from Allah (SWT) attest to this.

> *Allah (SWT) says: "And of no effect is the repentance of those who continue to do evil deeds until death faces one of them, and he says, now I repent, nor of those who die while they are disbelievers. For them, we have prepared a painful torment." (Quran 4:18)*

Asking for forgiveness should be a constant and consistent part of our lives as Muslims. Frequent contemplation of Allah's (SWT) lovely names keeps our hearts humble and in line with Allah's (SWT) divine direction. It supports us in staying spiritually pure and prepared to face our Creator with an open heart.

Names of Allah Related to forgiveness and Renewal

Consider using the following names from Asma ul Husna to ask for forgiveness and self-renewal:

Even though Allah (SWT) knows our transgressions and misdeeds, He pardons and welcomes sincere repentance. He is always forgiving and kind, regardless of the severity of the transgression. He loves to forgive and is the most forgiving. Using this name, we can rely on Allah's (SWT) boundless forgiveness and ask for His pardon for repeated transgressions.

There are various aspects of forgiveness, and it only humbles us when we fully understand what sin and forgiveness imply. We're all created to sin, according to Allah's (SWT) forgiving nature. The best people are not those who do not sin but seek repentance, own up to their errors, and ask Allah (SWT) for pardon. No matter what kind of sin a person has committed or how much they have committed, Allah (SWT) will forgive them if they seek genuine repentance. His mercy is greater than everything else.

Allah (SWT) is Al-Afuw, The Pardoner, the One who forgives sins and erases all evidence of wrongdoing. The distinction between effacing and forgiving is that the offence will neither be documented nor traced – it will appear as if it never occurred. For complete forgiveness of sins and a new beginning with a pure heart, invoke this name in your prayers.

He is Al-Afuw, the One who calls us to come back. He consistently leads people to repentance if they momentarily stray from the straight and narrow. Allah (SWT) is forgiving, restoring favour to those who turn from their sins and pardoning those who ask for it. After making mistakes, invoke this name to turn back to Allah (SWT), stressing real contrition and a commitment to growth.

The One who extracted a living human being from semen devoid of a soul is Allah (SWT), Al-Muhyi, The Giver of Life. On the Day of Resurrection, He will restore life by repairing our bodies and returning our souls. He is the one who illuminates people's hearts with the light of wisdom. Reflect on this name to uplift your soul and seek Allah's (SWT) assistance in reviving your purpose and faith.

Allah (SWT) is Al-Latif, The Subtle and Kind, who acts with such subtlety and kindness that His actions often go unnoticed. He is kind, loving, and perceptive of the finer details of each unique situation. His behaviour is so subtle that it's impossible to see or comprehend. You'll never know what He does for you. Call Allah (SWT) when you're in need of assistance, and ask for His subtle guidance and tender support to aid your inner healing and rejuvenation.

Allah (SWT) is Al-Quddus, The Most Holy, the One who is so far removed from all flaws and struggles with no shortcomings. He is so beyond any imperfection that even the mere statement that one is free from faults verges on offence. All of the exquisite qualities belong to Him, and He surpasses what we consider to be flawless. To purify your heart and work towards purity in your thoughts, intentions, and deeds, meditate on this name.

Ask Allah (SWT) for forgiveness and the fortitude to reaffirm your religion, morals, and life's purpose through these beautiful names.

Incorporating These Names into Personal Repentance and Self-Improvement

Incorporating the attributes of Allah (SWT) into personal repentance and self-improvement is a life-changing journey that can deepen your spiritual connection and foster meaningful personal growth. Each name of Allah (SWT) reflects a power and light that serves as a guide for believers to strive toward embodying qualities like compassion, wisdom, and justice. By reflecting on Asma ul Hasna, you can gain inspiration and strength to navigate the journey of repentance and self-betterment.

In the process of repentance (Tawbah), the Asma ul Husna provides a source of hope and motivation. For example, contemplating on Ar-Rahman, The Most Merciful, and Ar-Raheem, The Most Compassionate, reminds you of Allah's (SWT) boundless mercy, reassuring us that no sin is too great to be forgiven. Calling upon At-Tawwab, The Accepter of Repentance, and Al-Ghaffar (The Constant Forgiver) during prayers reinforces your faith in Allah's (SWT) readiness to accept your sincere efforts to return to Him. Meditating on these attributes can strengthen your resolve to leave behind harmful actions and make amends where possible.

For self-improvement, the Asma ul Husna offer an aspirational framework to emulate. By reflecting on Al-Adl, The Just, you can strive to practice fairness and justice in your interactions with others. Internalising As-Sabur, The Patient, can help you cultivate patience in the face of challenges, while Al-Hakim, The All-Wise, inspires you to seek wisdom in your decisions and actions. Each attribute serves as a lens through which you can assess your behaviour and work toward embodying higher virtues.

To practically incorporate the Asma ul Husna into your daily life, begin by selecting a few names to focus on based on your current challenges or goals. Recite and reflect on these names during your prayers, dhikr, or moments of contemplation. Journalling about how you can embody these attributes in specific situations can also be a powerful exercise. For example, if you struggle with anger, reflecting on Al-Halim, The Forbearing, may guide you toward a calmer response. Over time, aligning your actions with these divine qualities can lead to spiritual enrichment and personal transformation.

Chapter Four

Using the Names of Allah for Professional Development

Incorporating Divine Attributes into Work Ethics

Work ethic encompasses the beliefs and assumptions about the necessity of work – why it should be done – along with people's opinions on it and the methods used to motivate them to work. It also reflects an individual's attitude towards work, including their inclination for involvement and activity, their views on monetary and nonmonetary benefits, and their desire for professional advancement. All of these factors are extremely pertinent to contemporary analyses of working relationships in a market economy.

The sources of the Islamic work ethic or ideology are the Quran, the Sunnah (the sayings and actions of the Prophet (PBUH)), and the sayings and deeds of the Prophet's (PBUH) companions. The following terms are used in the Quran to describe its work ethic:

> *"And there is nothing for a person except what he strives for" (Quran 53:39)*

Nowadays, managers face daily challenges in ensuring a certain level of work ethic among employees in the office while maintaining morale and job satisfaction, especially as our understanding of the modern workplace and social behaviour continues to change. What was formerly believed to be a straightforward task that anyone could perform is now recognised as something far more complex that calls for knowledge, foresight, preparation, and a great deal of trial and error.

Many scholars have connected Islam's view of work and ethics in organisational settings to the lack of knowledge regarding organisational behaviour and management failure in many Muslim countries in the developing world. However, Islam is more than simply a religion; it's a way of life. As such, it offers its adherents a comprehensive set of work ethics that, when implemented in 21st-century organisations, have produced favourable outcomes.

At work, obtaining barakah (blessings) is just as important as reaching your necessary aims, goals, and KPIs to advance. Attaining barakah entails accomplishing your objectives without causing mental or emotional harm to others (yes, backstabbing is unacceptable). Rather, it's about sharing successful procedures, teaching and learning with those around you, and offering encouragement and support for others while doing so.

> *The Prophet (PBUH) stated: "Whoever relieves a Muslim of a burden from the burdens of the world, Allah will relieve him of a burden from the burdens on the Day of Judgement. And whoever helps ease a difficulty in the world, Allah will grant him ease from a difficulty in the world and in the Hereafter. And whoever covers (the faults of) a Muslim, Allah will cover (his faults) for him in the world and the Hereafter. And Allah is engaged in helping the worshipper as long as the worshipper is engaged in helping his brother." (Tirmidi)*

Islam has generated several useful examples that can be used as models for work ethics. For instance, Khadija bint Khwaylad (RA) was so impressed by Prophet Mohammed's (PBUH) honesty and sincerity in handling her financial concerns that she sent him a proposal for marriage.

Work ethics take on a whole new meaning when viewed as a duty for both social advancement and personal validation. An individual's comprehension of Islamic teachings will inevitably result in the satisfaction and fulfilment required for the accomplishment of organisational goals, even in situations where managers struggle to maintain employee morale.

We establish environments that strike a balance between accomplishing objectives and upholding moral principles by incorporating Allah's (SWT) qualities into business procedures, such as Al-Adl, The Just, to guarantee justice, Ar-Rahman, The Compassionate, to promote kindness, and Al-Mu'min, The Giver of Security, to establish trust. These values compel us to make sure that our actions positively impact other people's well-being while striving for perfection.

Essentially, connecting work ethics to the names of Allah (SWT) turns mundane professional duties into acts of worship. It encourages workers to strive for excellence, justice, and compassion, creating work environments where moral obligations and organisational goals coincide, eventually resulting in long-term success and peace in the workplace.

Using Names That Represent Justice, Honesty, and Excellence in Professional Conduct

A person's behaviour and conduct in a professional context are guided by a set of moral principles and values known as professional ethics. It includes several elements, including honesty, accountability, responsibility, and integrity. Working professionals must adhere to professional ethics in today's fast-paced and cutthroat environment to establish prosperous and long-lasting careers.

Professional values and ethics are the beliefs and principles that guide individuals in determining what is right and wrong in a professional setting. To put it succinctly, they represent the moral framework that a person upholds to support ethical behaviour in their profession.

These ethics and values are significant because they provide the foundation for professional conduct. These standards are used to assess an individual's or organisation's integrity and are recognised by both professional bodies and individuals. Promoting professional principles at various levels has several advantages: **Individual Level:** Ethical behaviour and ethical decision-making are guided by professional values and ethics, which can improve both our individual development and the standard of living in the community. Additionally, they support people's professional identities and performance, which boosts their self-confidence to work for a company.

Public Level: Establishing a shared definition of appropriate behaviour, professional ethics, and values increases trust in the reliability of the profession. When the norms of behaviour are made public, they also give customers and society members more transparency.

Business Level: Professional ethics and values can give a company a favourable reputation among customers, rivals, and the general public. They can offer a shared knowledge of appropriate behaviour, which increases an organisation's dependability. By setting expectations for proper conduct, they also contribute to the development of a welcoming and courteous workplace by minimising miscommunications amongst staff members.

Living up to the values represented by the names of Allah (SWT) shows true integrity and excellence. Al-Adl, The Utterly Just, calls for fairness and justice in decisions and actions and can be trusted. Al-Amin, The Trustworthy, reminds us of honesty and reliability for transparency in every interaction. These principles cultivate responsibility and vigilance, as one remains conscious of being accountable to Ar-Raqib, The Watchful, who observes all actions.

Similarly, the impartiality of Al-Hakam, The Impartial Judge, guides us to make decisions free from bias, reflecting fairness in every situation. Finally, Al-Muqsit, The Just One, stresses the importance of equity and balance, making one pursue excellence in the service of others with sincerity and hard work. Together, these attributes form a critical moral compass to uphold justice, honesty, and excellence in all professional initiatives.

Case Studies: How These Attributes Influence Workplace Behaviour

Here are some case studies illustrating how the attributes represented by Allah's (SWT) names can positively influence workplace behaviour:

Al-Adl (The Utterly Just): Promoting Fairness

Case Study: A project manager at a construction company notices that tasks are unevenly distributed among employees, leading to resentment and burnout. Guided by the principle of Al-Adl, the manager takes productive steps to redistribute the workload more equitably, ensuring everyone has a fair share, and the tasks are aligned with each individual's skills and capacity.

Outcome: Morale for the team improves, productivity increases, and the organisation builds a culture of equity and respect.

Al-Hakam (The Impartial Judge): Ensuring Unbiased Decision-Making

Case Study: A hiring manager must choose between two candidates—one is a personal acquaintance, and the other is more qualified. Motivated by Al-Hakam, the manager prioritises qualifications and selects the candidate best suited for the role.

Impact: The decision enhances team performance and builds confidence in the fairness of the company's recruitment process.

These examples demonstrate how embodying the principles of justice, honesty, and excellence can transform workplace behaviour.

Achieving Success Through Divine Guidance

One of Allah's (SWT) specific blessings that one must seek out is guidance (Hidayah). While we can ask Allah for many things – some of which He may grant or withhold according to His wisdom – guidance is not the same. Allah (SWT) will undoubtedly grant guidance if someone asks for it honestly, repeatedly, and with a pure heart. Our life here on Earth and in the Hereafter would be completely destroyed if Allah (SWT) hadn't guided us. This is why Allah's (SWT) instruction is so important in Islam.

Our lives become aimless and unfinished when we don't have Allah's (SWT) direction. Without Allah's (SWT) divine guidance, we cannot aspire to live a lovely and tranquil existence. His direction moulds our beliefs, choices, and deeds, guiding us towards a happy and purposeful life.

We discover meaning and clarity through this divine guidance, which empowers us to overcome obstacles and reach genuine fulfilment. The Holy Quran and Hadith place a great deal of emphasis on the significance of this guidance. The teachings of Prophet Muhammad (PBUH) and the words of Allah (SWT) give us a path for leading a life that pleases Allah (SWT) and is good for our souls.

Allah wants you to be successful, but it won't just fall into your lap like a cricket ball. He assured you that you would be rewarded for all your good deeds.

"The believers who are righteous will be fully rewarded." (Ale Imran)

Everyone aspires to success – be it in their spiritual, professional, or personal lives. As Muslims, we're aware that this is only possible with Allah's (SWT) assistance and direction. The Quran, as the divine source of wisdom, serves as a comprehensive guide for believers, enabling them to seek Allah's (SWT) direction in all facets of their lives.

Leveraging Names Related to Guidance and Success in Career Planning and Decision-making

Allah's (SWT) Beautiful Names (Asma ul Husna) can be invoked for guidance and success in career planning to bring spiritual clarity, motivation, and reliance on His Divine Wisdom. Below are some of the names of Allah (SWT) that relate very well to guidance and success, with ways to include them in your career planning and decision-making.

Al-Hadi (The Guide)

Allah (SWT) is Al Haadi means the One who provides direction to His followers. His advice is helpful and shields them from any dangers. To make sure that humanity is led in the correct direction, He is the one who sent prophets (PBUH) to communicate His message.

"Our Lord is He who gave each thing its form and then guided [it]." (Quran 20:50)

This ayah suggests that Allah's (SWT) counsel encompasses more than only pointing individuals in the direction of religion. There is more to it than that. Every element of a believer's life is infused with divine direction, which is given by Allah (SWT), the Al-Haadi. This advice affects daily judgements, moral judgements, and interpersonal relationships in addition to being saved for significant life decisions or spiritual awakenings.

> *"Indeed, my Lord is on a path [that is] straight."* (Quran 11:56)

Al-Fattah (The Opener, The Grantor of Success)

Al-Fattah is the opener, the revealer, and the giver of success. To whomever He pleases, He either opens or locks His doors of mercy. Everything confusing becomes plain under His direction. It is Allah (SWT) who has the finest judgement and the keys to success.

At some point in our lives, we've all faced situations where it felt like every road was blocked. It could be as minor as failing to grasp a challenging idea in class or as serious as consistently applying for jobs and never receiving a callback. It could also be as minor as attempting to contact someone or as serious as getting trapped in a depressive cycle. Every door you pass seems to be bolted, sealed, and locked with the most severe, most key-proof substance ever created.

In these moments, we are left with two choices. One possibility is that you continue to hit your head against the door, leaving yourself with nothing but a bruised forehead. The other is to approach Allah (SWT), the Best of Openers, whose infinite powers hold the key to unlocking the closed door in your path. Only by getting to know Allah (SWT), Al-Fattah, the Opener, can you discover the way forward.

Keep this in mind and apply this understanding in your daily life. Remember that one of Allah's (SWT) qualities is to be Al-Fattah, The Opener of the doors out of distress. Whenever you experience suffering, no matter how great or small, call upon Allah (SWT) using this name, seeking His help to relieve your pain.

Muslims are urged to seek Allah's (SWT) guidance in all aspects of life. This continuous relationship fosters a sense of direction and security and cultivates a faith-based dependence on Allah's (SWT) flawless wisdom to navigate life's challenges. It emphasises how crucial it is to maintain close contact with Allah (SWT) to make decisions that are in accordance with His desire.

Building a Positive Work Environment

A positive work atmosphere is critical to employee productivity and mental health, as well as the company's performance in today's world, where businesses strive to stay one step ahead of their rivals. Beyond comparison, a positive work atmosphere boosts employees' enthusiasm, morale, creativity, and productivity while contributing to greater job satisfaction.

In contrast, a negative workplace culture may affect a person's wellness and can have a major effect on a company's financial results by causing high turnover rates and low productivity. Conversely, employees at organisations with a positive corporate culture tend to be more content and efficient and less likely to quit.

As the saying goes, "Actions speak louder than words." Creating a strong ethical culture and embracing Islamic values in the workplace—such as justice, compassion, and honesty—also promotes respect, trust, and individual development. Adhering to Islamic beliefs and maintaining moral standards in your dealings with coworkers can foster a peaceful workplace and positively influence the people around you.

Names That Inspire Compassion, Understanding, and Teamwork

The beautiful names of Allah (Asma ul Husna) inspire values essential for compassion, understanding, and teamwork. Ar-Rahman (The

Most Merciful) and Ar-Raheem (The Most Compassionate) teach us boundless kindness, while Al-Wadud (The Most Loving) encourages love and unity. As-Salam (The Source of Peace) fosters harmony in group dynamics.

For understanding, Al-Alim (The All-Knowing) reminds us to seek knowledge and empathy, and Al-Hakim (The Most Wise) inspires wise decision-making. Ash-Shakoor (The Appreciative) promotes gratitude and mutual respect, while Al-Halim (The Forbearing) teaches patience. Together, these names encourage a spirit of collaboration, care, and mutual understanding in all interactions.

Balancing Faith and Work: Strategies for Muslim Professionals

The convergence of work and worship is a challenging balancing act for Muslim professionals, who must attempt to balance their religious and professional commitments. Keeping a strong religious connection becomes crucial as jobs grow and responsibilities rise. Let's look at doable tactics Muslim professionals might use to reconcile their religious and professional obligations.

Prioritise Allah (SWT): The cornerstone of our lives is our faith. It provides us with a feeling of purpose, moulds our values, directs our behaviour, and brings us inner serenity. By putting our connection with Allah (SWT) first, He, in turn, gives us the fortitude and resiliency we need to face challenges in other areas of our lives.

Remembering Allah (SWT) and the gifts He has bestowed upon us should be our top priority. Make time for everyday acts of praise, such as reading the Quran, performing dhikr, giving to charity, or lending a helping hand to someone in need, and try to pray on time. Allah (SWT) is the Most Merciful and loves us for our efforts, even if it's only a small amount each day.

The Prophet (PBUH) said, "Take up good deeds only as much as you are able, for the best deeds are those done regularly even if they are few." (Ibn Majah)

Communicating Openly with Employers: Regarding your religious commitments, keep lines of communication open and courteous with your employer. Discuss any adjustments or prayer breaks you require during fasting, such as Ramadan. Be upfront about your decision to abstain from alcohol and any physical concerns you may have, such as trembling hands. Many employers who understand and support religious beliefs create a favourable atmosphere for both work and worship.

Setting Priorities: Establishing priorities is essential to balancing work and religion. Islam emphasises the significance of carrying out both professional and religious duties, Putting religious obligations first, and having faith that Allah (SWT) will grant you success in your career.

Including Religion in Everyday Goals: Incorporate the aim to serve and uphold Islamic beliefs into your employment. Approach assignments with a spirit of quality, ethics, and commitment. Carry out your responsibilities diligently, striving to demonstrate your faith in your professional behaviour.

Maintaining a Healthy Work-life Balance: It's possible as a Muslim professional to manage your career while fostering your spiritual connection. When job searching, be sure to research the company's reputation and always look for businesses that will accommodate Muslims.

Chapter Five

Strengthening Relationships Using the Names of Allah

Improving Family Dynamics

The family is central to Islam and considered the cornerstone of society. The family unit plays a crucial role in raising individuals with good morals and showing them the right way. Islam strongly emphasises family values in its teachings. The institution of marriage between a man and a woman is central to the idea of a family, with the primary goal of providing a peaceful and morally sound setting for raising children.

Islamic family values, based on the teachings of the Prophet Muhammad (PBUH) and the principles set down in the Shariah, strongly emphasise passing down spiritual and moral principles from one generation to the next.

Some examples of these ideals are upholding the obligations and responsibilities stated in Islamic teachings, being polite and virtuous, and developing the qualities of a good Muslim.

Applying Names Related to Mercy, Love, and Patience in Family Interactions

Many of us are familiar with Allah's (SWT) many lovely names and qualities; some of us even commit to memorising them in an attempt to enter paradise. But how deeply do we actually understand these names, and how do they truly impact our lives?

Simply memorising a list of words is not beneficial if they don't actually affect our lives. So, let's reflect on some of Allah's (SWT) lovely names and explore how understanding their meanings can transform our lives and the lives of our families.

Integrating the names of Allah (SWT) that reflect mercy, love, and patience into family dynamics will have a resounding impact on the relationships that build a harmonious atmosphere. Here are some ways to implement these attributes:

Mercy (Ar-Rahman and Ar-Raheem)

Ar-Rahman denotes the attribute of Allah (SWT), the Glorified, whilst Ar-Raheem denotes its relationship to the object of mercy. Therefore, the former describes His essence, while the latter emphasises His mercy in action.

Together, these names convey that Allah's (SWT) benevolence is extensive and permeates every inch of the Creation in countless ways.

Allah's (SWT) endless acts of kindness towards His creation spread His love to all people and all creatures. We're blessed every day, whether it's in our family, health, wealth, sustenance, answered prayers, or even unseen favours.

We're also granted a chance to truly turn from our sins and become devoted followers of Him for the rest of our lives. We can never fully comprehend how much Allah (SWT) has favoured us in this life and bestowed upon us the invaluable gift of life.

Because everyone makes mistakes or has difficulties from time to time, families survive on mercy. Family members foster a secure and accepting environment where they can develop and learn from mistakes by exhibiting mercy.

Love (Al-Wadud)

The Beautiful Name Al-Wadud, often translated as The Most Loving, reflects that love is a component of Allah's (SWT) nature. Derived from the Arabic roots *wudd* or *widd*, which signify fondness or amity, Al-Wadud can alternatively be written as The Affectionate.

> *"Allah loves those who are constantly repentant and loves those who purify themselves." (Quran 2:222)*

Allah (SWT) doesn't need you, and you can't do Him any good. Nevertheless, He made you in the most ideal way possible to be who you are. Even when you don't realise it, He provides you with protection, love, education, guidance, and nourishment. Most significantly, He does this even if you reject Him.

Because He loves you, He never stops. Love in the world is frequently conditional. We love because we always receive something in return that fulfils us or helps us. However, the love of Allah (SWT) is unconditional and all-pervasive. You will fall in love with your Creator if you fully comprehend Allah's (SWT) benevolence and love for His creation.

Similarly, the cornerstone of a solid family is love. Verbal and physical displays of love strengthen ties and promote community. Hugs, nice words, and shared moments are examples of acts of love that strengthen emotional bonds and provide family members with a sense of worth and esteem. A caring and encouraging home can be established by routinely expressing affection to your spouse or complimenting your child on their hard work.

Patience (As-Sabur)

Allah (SWT) is As-Sabur, The Most Persistent and Patient One. He waits for the right moment and doesn't act rashly. Although He has the authority to punish wrongdoers, He gives us time to turn from our sins and modify our ways so that we can return to the correct path.

> *"O you, who believe, seek help through patience and prayer. Indeed, Allah is with the patient." (Quran 2:153)*

Allah (SWT) does not hasten to punish the careless and sinful. Instead, He shows patience when we veer off course, allowing us to find the correct path. As As-Sabur, He always keeps our path open because Saboor is the Most Persistent, Patient, and Enduring. He never rushes to do something before the right moment.

Despite rudeness and disobedience, Allah (SWT) is patient and continues to grant benefits and relief. Reflecting on Allah's (SWT) name, As-Sabur, allows us to derive a moral ethic. We can exercise patience in any situation if we remember Allah's (SWT) patience and how He treats people. By repeatedly exhibiting this quality, we develop the habit of being able to handle even the most trying situations with endurance and patience.

To handle disagreements, miscommunications, and the highs and lows of family life, patience is crucial. It keeps people from acting on impulse and enables them to respond thoughtfully while keeping the peace. Patience is frequently tested when raising children or handling domestic duties, but overcoming these difficulties with composure sets a good example.

Through the practice of pursuing these divine qualities, families improve not only their relationships with one another but also discharge an obligation in faith to imitate Allah's (SWT) mercy, love, and patience in everyday life.

Practical advice for using these attributes to strengthen familial bonds

Thus, good relations within the family may be entrenched and nurtured by modelling the attributes of Allah (SWT), which are mercy, love, and patience. When practised consciously, these qualities bring mutual respect, trust, and care into the home environment.

Mercy in family life means forgiving quickly and approaching mistakes with understanding. Suppose there is a situation where one family member forgets to do something important or makes a bad decision. The reaction of mercy toward the situation should be not angry but gentle: "It's okay, let's figure this out together." That will build trust and prevent resentment. Practice mercy, too, when correction is needed.

Children especially benefit from compassionate guidance. Instead of harsh reprimanding, explain calmly what went wrong and how to do it better next time.

Consistently expressing love strengthens the bonds within the family. Simple, comforting words like "I appreciate you" or "I love you" help family members feel valued. Demonstrative actions such as warm hugs, thoughtful love notes, or acts of service also communicate much love.

For example, surprising a spouse with their favourite meal or dedicating quality time to your children shows you care. In this way, emotional security and a feeling of belonging are created.

Patience is essential in navigating challenges and conflicts. Whether dealing with a child's repeated misbehaviour or managing disagreements with a spouse, staying calm and composed helps maintain harmony. Instead of reacting impulsively, take a moment to breathe, reflect, and respond thoughtfully. For instance, when teaching your child a new skill, be patient and encourage them, even if progress is slow. Your steadiness will set an example of perseverance and understanding.

The mercy and love of Allah (SWT), with patience, translate to living a compassionate, mutual-helping, and lasting bond within the family environment.

Enhancing Friendships and Social Connections

Your health and well-being can be significantly impacted by your friendships. However, establishing or maintaining friendships is not always simple. Recognise the value of social relationships in your life. Learn how to create and maintain enduring friendships.

As humans, we're able to survive and flourish because of our relationships with others. Whether it's in school, university, at work, or meeting other parents through our kids, life gives us the chance to make new friends without having to actively seek them out while we're younger.

Social interaction significantly impacts our mental and emotional health. When we connect with people, have meaningful conversations, and exchange experiences, we feel fulfilled and like we belong. This encourages an optimistic view of life and fights feelings of worry, despair, and loneliness.

Having a strong social network and meaningful relationships can greatly enhance our happiness and sense of fulfilment in life. When we have trusted friends with whom we can share our happiness and sorrows and celebrate life's milestones, we feel happier and more fulfilled, which improves our general well-being.

Unbelievably, social engagement also benefits our physical well-being. Participating in social activities and upholding solid social relationships can lower the risk of a number of illnesses, such as obesity, high blood pressure, and cardiovascular diseases. Additionally, it can strengthen our immune systems and extend our lives.

Additionally, friendships give life direction and significance. We participate in enjoyable activities and make enduring memories when we hang out with friends. This can offer us a sense of camaraderie and make us feel more confident and good about ourselves.

It's simple to become engrossed in our hectic lives in today's fast-paced world and neglect to prioritise our relationships. We can believe that we can get by without friends or that we don't have time for them. However, mental health issues like anxiety and depression can result from social isolation and loneliness.

Making excellent friends is very important in Islam since the people we spend time with can greatly influence our beliefs, behaviour, and deeds.

> *The Prophet Muhammad (PBUH) said: "A man is upon the religion of his best friend, so let one of you looks at whom he befriends." (Tirmidhi)*

Having good friends who are devoted to their faith can strengthen our religion and result in great spiritual growth. On the other hand, forming friendships with people who practise immorality or have weak faith might expose us to harmful influences and potentially sway us away from the straight and narrow.

Islam advises us to choose friends who are kind, caring, honest, trustworthy, and of high character. These are the sweet-smelling flowers or perfume vendors. These attributes support a healthy and constructive social environment and aid in our growth. In Islam, selecting close buddies is crucial. By supporting us in upholding our religious ideals and ideas, it can have a positive effect on our religion.

Names That Encourage Empathy, Support, and Trust in Friendships

The secret component that can revolutionise your relationships is empathy, which raises the bar for comprehension, connection, and support. The capacity to comprehend and experience another person's emotions, ideas, and experiences is known as empathy. It's more than pity, which is merely acknowledging someone else's feelings from a distance. By putting oneself in other people's shoes, empathy enables us to understand their perspective and establish a more profound emotional connection.

We all need friends who will genuinely listen to what we have to share on a daily basis. It might mean the difference between stagnation and progress. Such individuals, who are trustworthy observers of our stories, become the lubricants that keep our lives running smoothly, embodying empathy and understanding.

For those who are grieving, empathy is especially essential. Without the chance to share our story, sadness remains inside us and prevents us from healing. Grief, as we know, is complex and multifaceted, but at its core lies the need for others – people who accompany us on our journey, offering support and solace on our journey toward healing.

Similarly, genuine friendship requires the ability to rely on one another. Faith and confidence in your friends are crucial prerequisites for a solid connection. Respecting and keeping confidential what a friend tells you, regardless of its importance, is part of showing them that you care.

True friends listen with open ears and give counsel when requested, but they should never make fun of or laugh. Talking to a friend you can trust about a personal problem you're having and knowing that what you say will remain private and that they won't pass judgment on you or the situation is an example of having a trustworthy buddy.

Our personal development is influenced by the friendships we form throughout our lives. Your buddies can provide you with support, motivation, and company. They are probably among the most crucial individuals in your support network—people you can lean on in times of need.

Shared love, respect, and concern are common characteristics of supportive friendships. In these friendships, both parties contribute and receive equally. Mutual understanding is one of the most crucial elements of a strong friendship. It can be affirming to have a buddy who knows you well and values you for who you are; it gives you a feeling of acceptance and belonging.

The beautiful names of Allah (SWT) reflect His perfect attributes. Several of these names inspire qualities such as empathy, support, and trust, which can deepen friendships.

For example, Ar-Rahman, The Most Merciful, and Ar-Rahim, The Most Compassionate, remind us to be merciful, show deep compassion for others, develop understanding, and be kind in all our interactions.

Al-Wadud, The Most Loving, teaches us to establish relationships based on sincere love and personal warmth; Al-Karim, The Most Generous, is the inspiration to generosity with one's time, support, and words of encouragement. Al-Halim, The Most Forbearing, teaches us patience and tolerance to keep harmony and iron out any conflicts we may have.

Likewise, As-Salam, The Source of Peace, invites us to be sources of tranquillity and avoid causing harm or discord. At moments of hurt or misunderstanding, *Al-Ghaffar*, The Constant Forgiver, reminds us of the importance of forgiveness, letting go of grudges and rebuilding trust.

Al-Latif is a subtle and kind name that reminds us to be considerate of our friends' needs and feelings. An-Nasir encourages us to be reliable and supportive, particularly during hard times. Finally, Al-Adl, the Just, inspires fairness and integrity to build trust and mutual respect in a relationship. By reflecting on these divine attributes in our behaviour, we can cultivate compassionate, supportive, and deeply rewarding friendships.

Strategies for Nurturing and Maintaining Healthy Relationships

In Islam, establishing wholesome connections is important. For the sake of Allah (SWT), we're taught in our faith to cultivate solid and healthy relationships based on respect, kindness, and compassion for others. As a result, maintaining strong relationships can significantly influence many facets of our lives, benefitting not just ourselves but also people in our immediate vicinity. What are some strategies for creating these kinds of connections, then?

Love and kindness are the foundation of any successful relationship. Islam strongly focuses on the value of developing these traits in all kinds of relationships, including those with our families, spouses, friends, and the community.

> *"None of you [truly] believes until he loves for his brother that which he loves for himself." (Sahih Bukhari)*

This hadith serves as a reminder of our duty to treat our loved ones, neighbours, and community members with respect and compassion, upholding their rights and offering assistance when required. In his interactions with his companions, the Prophet (PBUH) also demonstrated this by urging them to look out for one another.

Any relationship will inevitably experience conflict, but how we handle and overcome it may make or ruin our bonds. Islam advises us to handle disagreement with discernment, tolerance, and modesty.

> *"The best of you are those who are best in character and the most patient in dealing with people." (Tirmidhi)*

There's a reason we've been given two ears and one mouth. Turn to the person and listen intently, as though you were the only two in the room, whenever they want to tell you a tale or simply chat. It goes without saying that you should avoid talking over them or being sidetracked. Pay close attention to the person speaking, occasionally nod and smile, ask a few pertinent questions, or offer your thoughts after they've finished. Make sure the person you're speaking to feels that you're paying attention to what they have to say.

In Islam, developing meaningful relationships requires empathy and compassion, which cannot be replaced.

> *"The parable of the believers in their affection, mercy, and compassion for each other is that of a body. When any limb aches, the whole body reacts with sleeplessness and fever." (Bukhari and Muslim)*

We learn from this hadith that compassion makes it possible for us to provide steadfast assistance. Developing empathy and compassion enables us to create nourishing and solid relationships, whether by listening to someone patiently or offering consolation to those going through a difficult time.

Developing wholesome relationships is a lifetime process that requires patience, commitment, and time. However, we can create deep ties that not only strengthen our community but also bring us closer to Allah (SWT) by practising kindness, empathy, compassion, and good communication.

Any relationship will inevitably experience conflict, but how we handle and overcome it may make or ruin our bonds.

> *"The best of you are those who are best in character and the most patient in dealing with people." (Tirmidhi)*

This hadith teaches us the value of patience and good character when interacting with others. When we have courteous, open discussions, carefully listen to others' viewpoints, and work towards understanding, we can handle disagreements with grace and compassion and turn them into opportunities for our relationships to grow.

By following these principles, individuals can maintain relationships that are not only harmonious but also deeply rooted in Islamic values.

Resolving Conflicts with Divine Wisdom

Conflict is a normal and natural part of life. For our interpersonal connections to succeed in the long run, we must learn how to handle disagreements. Relationship conflict often stems from personality conflicts or unfavourable emotional connections between two individuals. It can occur at home, in the workplace, or at social events.

While relationship conflict is a major source of stress and can be frustrating at times, unhealthy arguments can have a detrimental impact on both couples' physical and emotional well-being.

Everybody experiences conflicts in their lives, and we all need strategies to settle disputes amicably and effectively – whether with a coworker, spouse, or neighbour. For Muslims, Islam is the ultimate guide for navigating these challenges.

Using Allah (SWT) Names Associated with Peace and Reconciliation to Address and Resolve Conflicts

The names of Allah (SWT) are extremely significant and powerful, especially when they're employed to promote virtues like harmony, peace, and the ability to resolve conflicts. These are a few of His names that are especially significant for resolving disputes and promoting peace.

As-Salam (The Source of Peace)

Allah (SWT) is As-Salam. All of His creation is given peace and security by Him. Free from all frailties and sufferings, He is the origin of human security and tranquillity. Turning away from As-Salam leads to chaos and devastation. The reason those who are with Him experience is that He is perfect in all ways.

> *"He is Allah, and there is no Allah (SWT) beside Him, the Sovereign, the Holy One, the Source of Peace, the Bestower of security, the Protector, the Almighty, the Subduer, the Exalted. Holy is Allah, far above anything they associate with Him as His partners." (Quran 59:24)*

Being the All-Powerful Allah (SWT), Allah (SWT) is perfect and devoid of flaws. Peace is created by this lack of fault. He is the source and the giver of serenity since He is without fault. We must seek Allah's (SWT) assistance and obey His commands if we want true, lasting peace. He offers us security and comfort from stress and tension when we remember As-Salam and live in accordance with His instructions.

In the Quran, He informs us that our faith and memory of Him guarantee our hearts:

"Unquestionably, by the remembrance of Allah, hearts are assured." (Quran 13:28)

When we encounter challenges, we must remember that everything has a purpose because it originates from a flawless source. We might not fully comprehend the goal as we do not know everything. Even when it's not immediately obvious, we must have faith that wisdom and value can be gained from any circumstance. We shall find tranquillity by looking for advantages, cultivating thankfulness, and pleading with Allah (SWT) for assistance.

Al-Halim (The Forbearing)

When we harm someone, we pray for forgiveness, patience, and another opportunity. Humans are capable of tolerance; however, this forbearance may stem from feelings of helplessness, weakness, or a desire to avoid conflict. In contrast, Allah (SWT), who is self-sufficient and the source of all creation, honourably refers to Himself as Al-Ḥaleem, The Most Forbearing.

Being forbearing is more than just controlling your rage; it's about maintaining composure in the face of people who can control you or seek revenge. Therefore, Allah (SWT) attributes forbearance to Himself because it's a quality of strength, not weakness.

Allah (SWT) is the calmest, kindest, and most benevolent being, and not all sins are punished by Him. He is very kind and forgiving, and He tolerates. Even with the wrongdoers, He never acts rashly and always remains composed and thoughtful. He provides us with the chance to grow and show kindness.

One of Allah's (SWT) greatest gifts to us is His provision of rest. Instead of punishing us right away, He allows us time to repent and commit good deeds before we return to Him. Allah (SWT) not only postpones punishment but also gently reminds us to return to Him. In a similar vein, the earth and heavens ask for permission to exterminate the planet's inhabitants because of the severity of their transgressions. But because of His patience, Allah (SWT) forbids them from doing so:

> "Indeed, Allah keeps the heavens and the earth from falling apart. If they were to fall apart, none but Him could hold them up. He is truly Most Forbearing, All-Forgiving." (Quran 35:41)

In our interactions with Allah's (SWT) creation, we should strive to embody the same quality of forbearance if we wish to receive His tolerance. A forbearing individual remains composed and unfazed by the errors of others. He combines familial connections, smiles at people who scowl, makes explanations for other people's shortcomings, is quick to forgive, and resists the temptation to retaliate even if he has the right and power to do so. He has a big heart and is gentle. Despite our innate tendency to respond quickly, self-control and patience can be developed via practice.

> The Prophet (PBUH) said, "Knowledge comes through learning, and forbearance comes through practising forbearance." (Tabarani)

Indeed, conflict resolution does demand a proper mixture of divinely guided wisdom, patience, and understanding. Contemplation upon some of the magnificent names of Allah (SWT), As-Salam and Al-Halim, reminds us to embody peace and forbearance, respectively. Seeking guidance from Allah enables one to deal graciously with disputes for the sake of harmony in one's relationships. Challenges can thus be turned into opportunities when there is trust in His wisdom and self-restraint is practised. Ultimately, embracing these qualities at their highest divinity helps create a life rooted in peace and mutual respect.

Chapter Six

Overcoming Challenges and Stress with Divine Names

Finding Strength in Times of Difficulty

The world seems to be lurching from crisis to catastrophe lately. In addition to a variety of natural disasters, we have seen a worldwide pandemic, economic instability, political and social unrest, and significant shifts in the way we live our everyday lives.

People also have to deal with personal traumas, including losing a loved one, deteriorating health, being unemployed, getting divorced, experiencing violent crime, or suffering tragic accidents. This is a period of unheard-of hardship and turmoil for many of us.

Living during challenging times can significantly negatively impact your outlook, emotions, and health, regardless of whether the cause of the disturbance is a personal tragedy, a worldwide disaster, or both. You may feel powerless and overtaken by tension and worry as a result.

You might be experiencing intense grief over everything you've lost, be overcome by a wide range of challenging, contradictory feelings, or be unsure about how to keep going with your life. You can even think that everything in your life is entirely out of control, and you have no control over what might occur next.

Resilience is the capacity to handle trauma, grief, and change – challenges that have always been a part of life, even before these remarkable times. Developing resilience can help us navigate stressful situations, recover from adversity and tragedy, and adjust to life-altering events.

So, we frequently encounter challenging circumstances in life that test our limits. Relationship troubles, health concerns, or financial difficulties can all leave us feeling overburdened and apprehensive about the future. But our faith in Allah (SWT) is a strong source of hope and strength for Muslims.

It's crucial to avoid viewing your inability to handle hardship or misfortune as a sign of weakness. Resilience is a gradual process that takes work to develop and sustain throughout time; it's neither a fixed nor a tough trait.

It's unlikely that you've needed or had the chance to build resilience unless you've experienced adversity in the past. Using your former experiences as a guide will assist you in dealing with the difficulties you're currently encountering.

Even though it's frequently difficult to see any positive outcomes from traumatic events, developing resilience can help you find the good in the challenges you've encountered.

Overcoming adversity can help you learn valuable lessons about the world and yourself, fortify your determination, increase your empathy, and eventually allow you to develop and mature.

Allah (SWT) Names That Represent Strength, Resilience, and Patience During Challenging Times

There are obstacles and hardships in life. As Muslims, we know that this world will put us to the test.

> *Allah (SWT) says in the Quran: "We will certainly test you with a touch of fear and famine and loss of property, lives, and crops. Give good news to the steadfast." (Quran 2:155)*

Although hardship is unavoidable, how we handle it shows that we are. We can not only endure life's hardships but also get stronger as a result of cultivating patience and resilience. Patience in Islam refers to more than just perseverance. It's about remaining resilient and strong in the face of difficulties.

> *The Prophet (PBUH) said: "No one has ever been given anything better and more bountiful than patience." (Sahih Muslim)*

Resilience is the capacity to overcome hardship and recover from traumatic events. It involves becoming more resourceful, learning from mistakes, and adjusting to difficult situations. When we are resilient, we can handle life's inevitable challenges and uncertainties with emotional fortitude. Psychologists regard resilience as the secret to mental toughness.

Resilience and patience enable us to deal with hardship constructively. When faced with difficulties, patience helps us remain composed and hold fast to our beliefs. We have the fortitude to overcome obstacles and keep going when we are resilient. When taken as a whole, they keep us from losing hope or despair.

Being resilient and patient also allows us to help others facing comparable difficulties. We can be compassionate companions because of the empathetic knowledge we acquire from our own struggles. Our ability to bounce back from setbacks can be an example for friends, family, and neighbours.

The Quran and Sunnah offer direction and potent illustrations for developing patience in the face of hardship.

> *"Indeed, with hardship [will be] ease." (Quran 94:6)*

> *"And be patient, [O Muhammad], and your patience is not but through Allah. And do not grieve over them and do not be in distress over what they conspire. Indeed, Allah is with those who fear Him and those who are doers of good." (Quran 16:127-128)*

During challenging times, several names of Allah (SWT) embody strength, resilience, and patience, offering comfort and guidance. Al-Aziz (The Almighty, The Invincible) reminds us of Allah's (SWT) unparalleled power and control over all matters, while Al-Qawiyy (The Strong) reflects His immense strength, encouraging believers to seek support from Him during hardships.

As-Sabur (The Patient) highlights Allah's (SWT) attribute of patience, inspiring us to endure trials with steadfastness. Al-Hafiz (The Preserver) reassures us of His protection and care, even in the most trying circumstances. Similarly, Al-Mateen (The Firm One) symbolises Allah's (SWT) unwavering firmness, instilling resilience in our hearts.

Trust in Allah's (SWT) provision is reinforced by Ar-Razzaq (The Provider), while Al-Mujib (The Responsive One) assures us that He hears and answers the prayers of those who turn to Him. Relying on Al-Wakil (The Trustee, The Disposer of Affairs) reminds us of Allah's (SWT) wisdom in managing everything for our ultimate good. Furthermore, Al-Latif (The Subtle and Kind) reflects Allah's (SWT) gentle care, even when His wisdom is beyond our comprehension. Finally, An-Nasir (The Helper) reassures us of His aid in times of need. Meditating on these names and invoking them in dua can provide spiritual strength, peace, and hope during life's challenges.

Cultivating Patience and Perseverance

Perseverance and patience (sabr) are recurrent themes in the Quran and are highlighted as crucial qualities for believers. These traits are not only praised but also promoted as essential for conquering obstacles in life and attaining spiritual development. Many thoughts on patience and tenacity can be found in the Quran, offering direction and support to those going through difficult times.

One of the qualities that is most highly regarded and emphasised in Islam is sabar. Sabar, which comes from the Arabic root word Sabr, is a profound concept that goes beyond mere patience; it also means tenacity, fortitude, persistence, and perseverance. Sabar teachings in Islam exhort believers to be steadfast in their faith and self-control, to avoid giving in to frustration, and to be thankful even in the face of adversity. In Islam, Sabar is an active aspect of a believer's spiritual path rather than just a passive endurance, demonstrating the close relationship between faith, endurance, and personal development.

> *"O you who have believed, seek help through patience and prayer. Indeed, Allah is with the patient." (Quran 2:153)*

This verse emphasises the value of patience as a proactive practice in one's spiritual journey and a way to deal with hardship.

Another important subject in the Quran is steadfastness, or perseverance (Istiqamah), which represents the determination to uphold one's moral principles and faith in the face of difficulties and temptations. Perseverance is frequently linked to achievement and divine favour in the Quran.

> *Allah (SWT) says, "And be patient, for indeed, Allah does not allow the reward of those who do good to be lost." (Quran 11:115)*

This verse highlights the long-term advantages of perseverance and reassures believers that their efforts will not be in vain.

The Quran offers helpful advice on how to develop endurance and patience in daily life. It exhorts Muslims to ask for assistance through prayer, remember Allah (SWT), and maintain an optimistic outlook.

Names That Embody Patience and Perseverance

In Islamic tradition, several of Allah's (SWT) names from the Asma ul Husna reflect qualities of patience, perseverance, and steadfastness. These include:

As-Sabur (The Most Patient): Allah (SWT) is the epitome of patience, delaying punishment for wrongdoers and granting countless opportunities for repentance and forgiveness.

Al-Halim (The Forbearing): Allah (SWT) does not hasten to punish despite human transgressions. His forbearance embodies restraint and tolerance.

Ar-Rahman (The Most Merciful): His mercy and compassion demonstrate His endurance and love for creation, even in the face of disobedience.

Al-Ghaffar (The Constant Forgiver): Allah's (SWT) constant forgiveness is a sign of His perseverance in bestowing His mercy upon His servants.

Ar-Razzaq (The Sustainer): Allah (SWT) continuously provides for all creation, embodying the persistence of care and provision.

These names encourage believers to cultivate patience and perseverance, trusting Allah's (SWT) wisdom and timing.

Techniques For Incorporating These Attributes Into Daily Struggles

Incorporating the divine attributes of patience and perseverance into daily struggles requires intentional reflection and practical actions inspired by these qualities. Here are some techniques:

Practice periods: Try enforcing practice periods where you actively focus on cultivating patients. Make niyyah (intention) and sincerely ask Allah (SWT) to grant you more patience in certain areas. After all, according to reports, Ali ibn Abi Talib stated: "To be patient is to ask Allah (SWT) for assistance."

Control your emotions: Learn to pause and manage your emotions, especially when faced with difficult circumstances. This break gives you time to reflect and react sensibly. Recognise that difficulties are a part of a larger plan and are only transitory. Pay more attention to the bigger picture than to your current misery.

Stay focused on your responsibilities: You're probably not paying attention to your work, your religious practice, or anything that brings you joy when you're angry about your problems or impatient for your life to turn out the way you want it to. This will simply make you feel more anxious, which will probably make you feel depressed.

Allah (SWT) wants you to be responsible for your obligations in life, even though He also wants you to turn to Him at these times. Your work, maintaining your house, and looking after your parents, kids, or anyone else you are responsible for. You'll feel much more depressed if you neglect these responsibilities and instead mope anxiously. When you're in this situation, it becomes increasingly harder to believe that Allah (SWT) will make things right in your life, and you risk growing further and further away from Him.

View challenges as a test: Allah (SWT) is responsible for everything that happens to you, both good and evil. These are supposed to be tests. For instance, receiving financial blessings and being judged by how you use them. Are you putting others' needs ahead of your own? On the other hand, you are being put to the test when you encounter adversity. During these hardships, will you walk away from Allah (SWT), or will you remember and trust His wisdom?

Seek guidance and support: Consult the Quran or the sayings of Prophet Muhammad (PBUH) for Allah (SWT)'s instructions on becoming more patient. Visit a nearby mosque and look for knowledgeable individuals who can offer you advice if you feel like you need it. Or just ask your friends to pray with you and support you. Help is always available if you seek it out.

Remember that patience is difficult. So don't worry if it appears almost impossible to be patient, concentrate on prayer, and turn to Allah (SWT) even when things are difficult. Allah (SWT) is fully aware of your difficulties and the effort you put into turning to Him patiently and asking for His assistance.

Seeking Relief and Comfort

Everything that the Almighty chooses for us in life is well-balanced and ideal. Allah (SWT) knows the logic behind why we are put through difficulty, and if we know it, He occasionally reveals it to us.

As believers, we realise that whatever Allah (SWT) decides for us is the best, especially as we learn more about our deen. We understand that everything in life is a test, good and bad, appealing and displeasing. Therefore, despite the difficulties we encounter, we should never give up. It's crucial that we respectfully ask Allah (SWT) for His consolation and protection throughout difficult and painful situations.

> *Allah (SWT) says in the Quran: "If only, when our calamity came upon them, they humbled themselves. But their hearts hardened, and Shaytan made their deeds appear good to them." (Quran 6:43)*

Names Associated with Comfort, Solace, and Peace

In Islamic tradition, many of Allah's (SWT) names are connected to peace, comfort, and tranquillity. These names are a reflection of His kindness, compassion, and capacity to calm people's emotions. The following names are specifically linked to these attributes:

Al-Mu'min (The Giver of Faith and Security): Allah (SWT), as Al-Mu'min, provides safety, faith, and assurance to His creation. This name signifies that Allah (SWT) instils a sense of peace and security in the hearts of those who believe in Him. He is the ultimate protector from fear, anxiety, and harm, offering spiritual and emotional solace to His servants. Turning to Al-Mu'min helps believers find tranquillity, knowing that He safeguards their well-being.

Al-Karim (The Generous): Al-Karim reflects Allah's (SWT) infinite generosity and boundless giving. He bestows blessings abundantly, often without us even asking. His generosity is not limited to material provisions but extends to guidance, forgiveness, and opportunities for spiritual growth. Understanding Allah (SWT) as Al-Karim reassures believers that He provides all they need and that His kindness and care are always present, bringing comfort and hope.

Al-Hadi (The Guide): As Al-Hadi, Allah (SWT) guides His creation toward truth, righteousness, and a life of peace. He illuminates the hearts of those who seek Him, helping them navigate life's challenges and uncertainties. Through His guidance, believers find purpose and direction, which leads to inner peace and contentment. Reflecting on Al-Hadi inspires trust in Allah's (SWT) wisdom and encourages reliance on Him for clarity and resolution. Each name offers unique comfort and assurance, emphasising Allah's (SWT) active role in providing peace, sustenance, and guidance.

Importance of Supplication

It's impossible to exaggerate the significance of praying to Allah (SWT). Dua, as described by the renowned Imam Ibn al-Qayyim, is among the most effective remedies. It's the enemy of disaster; it wards it off, heals it, stops it from happening, and, if it does, it lessens or eases it [one]. It is the believer's weapon. As Muslims, we have been endowed with strong and potent duas that can help us become closer to Allah (SWT) while also relieving tension and worry. You can recite these five brief but powerful duas every day to help you stay composed and find comfort during these trying times:

> *"O Allah, I take refuge in You from anxiety and sorrow, weakness and laziness, miserliness and cowardice, the burden of debts and from being overpowered by men."*
> *(Al-Bukhari)*

This prayer is especially crucial during tumultuous times of broad economic instability, public health emergencies, and general anxiety about the future. A believer might find comfort in this prophetic prayer and use their faith to keep hope alive and avoid terror. They are aware that the Most Merciful Protector and Wise Overseer will protect anybody who seeks refuge in Allah.

> *"Allah is enough for me. There is no true Allah (SWT) but Him, in Him I put my trust, and He is the Lord of the Great Throne." (Abu Dawud)*

Repeat seven times. This dua serves as a reminder that Allah (SWT) controls everything in the universe. Our hearts can be calmed by our faith in Him and His divine plan. We are free from concern once we've worked hard to achieve our goals. The Lord of "the Great Throne," the greatest creation of all, will decide the outcome.

> *"O Allah, I hope for Your mercy. Do not leave me to myself even for a blink of an eye. Correct all of my affairs for me. There is none worthy of worship except You." (Bukhari)*

One of the prayers for those in distress is this dua. Fatima (RA), his daughter, was counselled by the Prophet (PBUH) to recite it both in the morning and at night. When you place your trust in Allah (SWT), your affairs will be taken care of; thus, you're pleading with Him not to abandon you.

You are calling upon the One who continuously oversees the activities of the world, imploring Him not to abandon you because you might make mistakes, follow your wants, or lack discernment. In times of difficulty, turn to Allah's (SWT) with full faith in His mercy, trusting that He will resolve all of your issues. There's nothing better than knowing that Allah (SWT) is always there for you. The ultimate source of peace is Allah (SWT).

We encounter a variety of challenges throughout our lives that put our fortitude and resiliency to the test. However, faith can play a crucial role in fostering our mental health. Particularly in the Quran, Allah (SWT) exhorts us to rely on our faith, community support, and faith in Him to overcome our difficulties.

> *"Say, 'Nothing will ever befall us except what Allah has destined for us. He is our Protector.' So in Allah let the believers put their trust." (Quran 9:51)*

This passage is a helpful reminder to trust Allah (SWT) and rely on Him for protection, strength, and direction during trying times.

Chapter Seven

Enhancing Spiritual Connection through the Names of Allah

Deepening Your Relationship with Allah (SWT)

As Muslims, it's essential to cultivate a close relationship with Allah (SWT) because this bond is crucial for our success in this world and the next. We need to get in touch with our Creator. He only wants the best for us, both here on Earth and in the afterlife. Have you ever witnessed your mum showing you love? Can you even begin to comprehend how much Allah (SWT) loves us? Nobody is unable to. The depth of His love surpasses anything we can imagine.

You may sometimes question your mother's feelings for you, but can you ever doubt the purity of her affection or her good intentions towards you?

Now focus on this: Allah (SWT) loves us seventy times more than a mother loves her child. Yes, He loves us that much—not once, not twice, but seventy times. We establish a connection with our mother, correct? No matter what, we must talk to our mothers whenever we're feeling low, depressed, or joyful. Therefore, developing a relationship with Allah (SWT) is far more significant than we may think. He loves you more than anyone else can. And no one has the same best interests for you in mind as He does. Give him a central place in your life. And see the distinction.

Islam serves as a ray of hope, direction, and a reminder for people aware of the ultimate objective, the Akhirah, or eternal life, in this world, which is characterised by the evidence of its transient nature and the attraction of its diversions. The Quran reminds us of our ultimate goal in life in a number of places as we make our way through the general gloom of this world.

> *Allah (SWT) states: "And we did not create the jinn and mankind except to worship me."(Quran 51:56)*

Allah (SWT) does not suddenly grow distant from your heart; rather, it's a gradual process. It begins by becoming slack in your worship, putting off prayer, and disparaging your transgressions. When you start to feel as though you don't really have a purpose in life, the joys of this world take precedence over all other concerns, and some sins turn into habits that you can't seem to break.

> *The Messenger (PBUH) said: "There lies within the body a piece of flesh. If it is sound, the whole body is sound and if it is corrupted, the whole body is corrupted. Verily this piece is the heart." (Sahih Muslim)*

As Muslims, we recognise the value of having a close relationship with Allah (SWT). Developing a close relationship with our Creator that may significantly influence our lives is more important than merely following rituals.

We must first get to know Allah (SWT) to have a heart that is connected to Him. How can we hope to establish a solid bond with someone we don't know well? The Quran is one of the ways Allah (SWT) granted us to do this. Spending time studying and considering His Names, which we learn from the Quran and Sunnah, is another way to get to know Him.

> *The Prophet (PBUH) said: "Allah the Almighty said: I am as my servant thinks I am. I am with him when he mentions me. If he mentions me to himself, I mention him to myself; and if he mentions me in an assembly, I mention him in an assembly greater than it. If he draws near to me a hand's length, I draw near to him an arm's length. And if he comes to me walking, I go to him at speed." (Sahih Muslim)*

Recognise that Al-Khaliq, the One who created us and everything we could possibly want, is Allah (SWT), Al-Qadir, the One who can do anything, regardless of how unattainable it may appear to our finite senses; As-Sami', the One who hears all of our prayers. Understanding these attributes helps us establish a constructive framework for our relationship with Allah (SWT), one that we're willing to work on and invest in.

We learn from His Names that He is The Source of Peace (As-Salam), The Source of Love (Al-Wadud), and He is Merciful. But as soon as we make a mistake, we frequently have a tendency to give up.

This is frequently the cause of our complete disconnection from Allah (SWT); Allah (SWT) does not seek out excuses to punish, reject, or drive us away. He is searching for reasons to accept and be there for us when no one else is.

We have the five daily prayers in accordance with the remembrance of Allah (SWT), but we have also been given the Quran, which was sent down to be read, lived, and engaged with daily rather than merely being placed on our shelves. In the Quran, Allah (SWT) states that remembering Him brings us the utmost peace and tranquillity. The Quran is crucial to maintaining the firmness of our hearts because it's considered the best form of memory.

Reflecting on the Meanings of the Names to Strengthen Spiritual Connection

Reflecting on the meanings of the names of Allah (SWT) provides us with a power that deepens our spiritual connection and increases awareness of Allah's (SWT) presence in our lives. In Islam, each name of Allah (SWT) defines an aspect of His divine nature, mercy, and attributes. By contemplating and understanding the attributes and their meanings, we can draw ourselves closer to Allah (SWT) and develop a stronger sense of devotion.

Let's have a look at a few names of Allah (SWT). For example, Al-Malik (The King) calls one to ponder Allah's (SWT) sovereignty and how each and everything in the universe is working under His rule. Meanwhile, Al-Quddus (The Most Sacred) reminds us that He is the best in His purity and holiness, transcending everything in the created world.

Reflection and a deep understanding of these names assist us to have a deeper appreciation of Allah's (SWT) attributes and how they manifest in the world around us.

Contemplating the names of Allah (SWT) also offers an opportunity for personal application. For example, when reflecting on Al-Ghaffar (The Constant Forgiver), one can think about the times they have sought Allah's (SWT) forgiveness and how He has granted them with mercy. This reflection can foster a sense of peace, gratitude, and humility.

Similarly, understanding Al-Razzaq (The Provider) encourages gratitude as you reflect on the many blessings and sustenance Allah (SWT) has given you. These reflections help strengthen your connection to

Allah (SWT) by reminding you of His constant presence and mercy in your life.

As mentioned earlier, incorporating Allah's (SWT) names into your supplications (duas) is another meaningful way to reflect on His attributes. For example, when seeking Allah's (SWT) help or guidance, you might invoke Al-Wahhab (The Supreme Bestower) or Al-Latif (The Subtle One, the Kind).

Using these names in your prayers connects the name and your heartfelt request, reinforcing the understanding that Allah (SWT) is the source of all blessings and mercy.

Reflecting on the names of Allah (SWT) also cultivates a deep sense of trust and reliance on Him. Names such as Al-Wakeel (The Trustee) and Al-Qadir (The Omnipotent) remind you that Allah (SWT) has control over all matters. By trusting His wisdom and power, you recognise you're never alone in your challenges. This trust nurtures a sense of peace and surrender, knowing that Allah (SWT) is always in control.

Finally, engaging in continuous remembrance (dhikr) of Allah's (SWT) names helps keep your heart focused and connected to Him. Repeating the names aloud or in your heart can bring comfort, clarity, and a sense of peace to your mind.

This practice strengthens your spiritual connection, providing a constant reminder of Allah's (SWT) presence in your daily life.

Daily Practices and Supplications Involving the Names of Allah (SWT)

Understanding and applying the names that Allah (SWT) has chosen to disclose to us via the Quran and Sunnah is the first step towards loving Him. Using His lovely names and traits in our duas is one of the best methods to reinforce our understanding of them. Look for a quality in your Lord that fits each requirement you have.

Al-Wakeel (The Disposer of Affairs)

When you're short on time, funds, or resources, give Al-Wakeel a call. Put your faith in Allah (SWT) and say: *Hasbunallah wa ni'mal wakeel (Sufficient for us is Allah and [He is] the best Disposer of Affairs)*

Al-Mujeeb (The One Who Responds)

Call on Al-Mujeeb if you're in dire need of assistance, upset, or facing significant challenges.

> *The Prophet (PBUH) said, "Allah is conscientious and generous. He is shy to return the outstretched hands of his servant empty and disappointed." (Tirmidhi)*

Al-Jabbar (The Restorer)

When you discover you cannot accomplish a task, ask Al-Jabbar to help make a difference. How flawless He is, with absolute power, dominion, majesty, and magnificence

Al-Wali (The Protecting Friend)

Call Al-Wali if you need someone to help you get out of trouble:

> *"You are our Protector, so forgive us and have mercy upon us. You are the best of those who forgive." (Quran 7:155)*

Al-Shafi (The Healer)

Whatever ailment you or a loved one is experiencing, call on Al-Shafi:

> *"O Allah, Lord of the people! Remove the trouble and heal the patient, for You are the Healer. There is no healer but You; give him a healing which leaves no disease behind." (Sahih Bukhari)*

In conclusion, we can strengthen our relationship with Allah (SWT) by introducing His lovely names and qualities into our regular prayers and activities. We strengthen our faith and welcome His kindness, protection, and direction into our lives by comprehending and using these names.

Incorporating Names into Worship and Prayer

Knowing Allah's (SWT) names turns into a personal act of devotion that encourages followers to contemplate, comprehend, and absorb the essence of Allah (SWT). It's a spiritual activity that helps people feel more connected to and aware of Allah (SWT)'s presence in everyday life.

So, how does one start this quest to understand Allah (SWT)? It begins with the Quran, where these names are woven throughout its verses to give each quality depth and significance.

Consider Al-Wadud (The Loving) as an example.

> *The Quran states, "And He is the Forgiving, the Loving" (Quran 85:14)*

Emphasising that Allah's (SWT) forgiveness is a guarantee for those who seek comfort in His kindness and that His love is accompanied by it. Invoke these names in your frequent dhikr and dua to feel closer to Allah (SWT) each time.

The life and teachings of the Prophet Muhammad (PBUH), who demonstrated the qualities of Allah (SWT) via his actions, also provide insight into the meaning of each name. Making the Seerah a regular read is worthwhile because his sayings and deeds were tangible examples of Allah's (SWT) attributes, directing Muslims to live by these admirable standards.

Knowing Allah's (SWT) names helps us appreciate and adore Him more because it provides a glimpse into His boundless majesty and mercy. Memorising the Quran, where each verse brings one closer to Allah (SWT), is the ideal complement to this voyage of love and wisdom. Islam holds that incorporating Allah's (SWT) names into prayer and devotion is a spiritual practice that strengthens believers' bonds with the Almighty.

How to Use the Names of Allah (SWT) in Personal and Communal Prayers

One technique to improve the efficacy of worship and deepen one's relationship with the Divine is to use the names of Allah (SWT) in both private and public prayers. Muslims can use Allah's (SWT) names both individually and collectively to ask for direction, mercy, and blessings, as well as to consider the qualities of Allah (SWT) that are most pertinent to their needs and situations. The names of Allah (SWT) can be used in both private and public prayers in the following ways:

Through Prayer: Invoking Allah's (SWT) names in prayers and supplications is one of the best methods to strengthen spiritual connections on a daily basis. By calling upon particular names that speak to their present needs or circumstances, Muslims might strengthen their spiritual ties. For example, when asking for forgiveness, one could invoke Al-Ghaffar (The All-Forgiving), recognising Allah's (SWT) infinite forgiveness and urging oneself to repent regardless of one's transgressions.

Similarly, in times of difficulty or uncertainty, invoking Ar-Razzaq (The Provider) or Al-Muhaymin (The Protector) can bring comfort to believers in difficult or uncertain circumstances. These names give the faithful hope and patience by reminding them of Allah's (SWT) unwavering provision and care.

Aligning Supplications with Particular Names of Allah (SWT): Muslims can dedicate a specific period of time each day to contemplate the significance and consequences of a particular name of Allah (SWT) in their lives. For example, calling upon Al-Adl (The Just) or Al-Latif (The Subtly Kind) during times of distress can provide hope and a sense of divine support.

Drawing Strength and Guidance: Muslims can look to particular names of Allah (SWT) for courage and inspiration when they are struggling or looking for direction. For example, when starting a new project, one could call upon Al-Fattah (The Opener) to ask Allah (SWT) to assist them in breaking through barriers and opening doors of opportunity. In a similar vein, calling upon Al-Musawwir (The Fashioner) might serve as a reminder to those pursuing self-improvement of Allah's (SWT) ability to guide and direct people towards their best selves.

Here are some ways to incorporate Allah's (SWT) names into personal prayers:

Direct Invocation: Begin your dua by calling upon specific names of Allah (SWT) that reflect your need or request. For example:

- When seeking guidance: Use "Ya Hadi" (O Guide) to ask for guidance in making decisions or navigating life's challenges.
- When seeking forgiveness: Say "Ya Ghaffar" (O Forgiver) to invoke Allah's (SWT) mercy for forgiveness.
- When seeking protection: Call upon "Ya Mu'min" (O Giver of Security) to ask Allah (SWT) to protect you from harm or danger.

- When in distress: Invoke "Ya Rahman" (O Most Merciful) or "Ya Rabb" (O Lord) to seek comfort and Allah's (SWT) mercy and help in times of difficulty.

Using Names in Duas for Specific Needs: When making Dua for a particular need, choose the name of Allah (SWT) that aligns with that need:

- For provision: Call upon "Ya Razzaq" (O Provider) to request sustenance and provision.
- For patience: Use "Ya Sabur" (O Patient One) to seek Allah's (SWT) for patience in times of trials.
- For strength: Invoke "Ya Qawi" (O All-Strong) to ask for Allah's (SWT) help to stay strong in difficult times.

Using Allah's (SWT) Names in Communal Prayers

Communal prayers (Salah) have a collective aspect, but Allah's (SWT) names can still be incorporated in various ways to enhance the congregation's experience and worship. Here's how they can be used:

Opening Supplications in Congregational Prayers: Before or after the prescribed prayers (Salah), an imam or the congregation can recite supplications that invoke Allah's (SWT) names. Some examples include:

- "Bismillahir Rahmanir Rahim" (In the name of Allah (SWT), the Most Gracious, the Most Merciful) – recited at the beginning of Surah Al-Fatiha and before initiating any important action.
- "Allahumma, Ya Rahman, Ya Raheem" (O Allah, O Most Merciful, O Most Compassionate) – invoking Allah's (SWT) mercy for the entire community.

Special Prayers in Congregational Settings: In special communal prayers, like Salat al-Tarawih (during Ramadan), the imam may invoke the names of Allah (SWT) while making dua for the community:

- "Ya Qadir" (O All-Powerful) – seeking strength and resolve for the community.

- "Ya Wali" (O Protecting Associate) – calling upon Allah (SWT) for protection and guidance for the Muslim ummah (community).

Reciting Allah's (SWT) names during personal and congregational prayers serves as a means for believers to remember Allah's (SWT) attributes, implore His mercy, and base their supplications on those attributes. Reciting the Names of Allah (SWT) singly or in congregation strengthens one's connection with Allah (SWT), directs and guides the believer in worship, and invokes peace and blessings upon the individual and the community.

Personalising Your Spiritual Practice

Spiritual activities hold a long-standing and significant role in psychology, recognised for their capacity to foster resilience, personal development, and well-being. A number of methods support people's psychological health, inner tranquillity, and social discomfort. Islamic teachings and the traditions of the Prophet Muhammad (PBUH) serve as the foundation for spiritual practices in Islamic psychology.

Promoting psychological well-being, inner serenity, and a stronger relationship with the all-powerful Allah (SWT) is the primary goal of such practices. Salah (prayer), tawbah (repentance), dhikr (memory of Allah SWT), fasting, sadaqah (charity), and sabr (patience) are a few instances of Quranic spiritual practices.

While spirituality entails a relationship with the natural world and the universe that eventually leads to Allah (SWT), religion entails relationships, service, and worship of Allah (SWT). Being exposed to your religion and Allah (SWT) and having personal experiences are all part of being spiritual. Religion, on the other hand, is the belief in experience.

Spirituality originates in your soul and is not based on any philosophy or doctrine. Religion is a viewpoint, but spirituality is always present. We are connected to the universe and the highest force, Allah Almighty (SWT), through the network of spirituality.

Spiritual practice in Islam is crucial because it forms the essence of a Muslim's relationship with Allah (SWT) and guides every aspect of life. Here's why it holds immense importance:

Strengthening Connection with Allah (SWT): Through spiritual practices like prayer (Salah), fasting (Sawm), and supplication (Dua), Muslims develop a close and intimate relationship with Allah (SWT). These exercises foster inner serenity and mindfulness in day-to-day living while strengthening one's relationship with Allah (SWT).

Foster Regular Worship: To strengthen their spiritual ties, Muslims are urged to develop a regular prayer schedule and participate in voluntary prayers, also known as Sunnah prayers. Furthermore, setting aside time every day for Quranic reflection and recitation fosters spiritual insight and faith.

> "O believers! Seek comfort in patience and prayer. Allah is truly with those who are patient." (Quran 2:153)

The five daily prayers (Salah) are a fundamental act of worship for all Muslims. Before the real prayer begins, ablution is performed, followed by supplications, recitation of Quranic verses, intention, attentiveness, and physical gestures.

Fajr (two rakaah in the early morning), Zuhr (four rakaah at noon), Asr (four rakaah at midday), Magrib (three rakaah at early night) and Isha (four rakaah at night) are the five daily prayers.

Establishing a direct line of communication and relationship with Allah (SWT), asking for His direction, and finding peace in His memory are the primary goals of prayer (Salah). Allah (SWT) directed the Prophet Muhammad (PBUH) to "recite what is revealed to you of the Book and establish prayer," according to the Quran (29:45). Indeed, prayer increases one's memory of Allah (SWT) and forbids immorality and wrongdoing. And Allah (SWT) is aware of all you do.

The Quran as a Guide: The Holy Quran is a divine blessing, and Muslims are encouraged to approach the Quran and develop a closer, more intimate relationship with it. Muslims who become enthralled with the potent words of the Creator of nature might succeed by understanding the actual meaning of Quranic verses and putting them into practice in their daily lives.

The Power of Dua and Dhikr: Another way to communicate directly with Allah (SWT) is through Dua and Dhikr. When performing these practices, Muslims should feel it deep in their heart. Allah (SWT) answers those who call upon Him and remembers those who remember Him.

Creating a Personalised Approach to Using the Names in Spiritual Routines

There are many different instruments, both material and intangible, that you can use to explore your spirituality. You also have complete control over the frequency, timing, and intensity of specific practices because it's a very self-directed process. Some tools and practices for your spiritual practice are listed below.

Identify Your Intention: Reflect on what you seek to achieve with your spiritual practice. For example: Inner peace? Strength in times of difficulty? A deeper connection to Allah (SWT)?

Choose names of Allah (SWT) that resonate with your goals. For example, if seeking mercy, reflect on Ar-Rahman (The Most Merciful) and Ar-Raheem (The Most Compassionate). For guidance, focus on Al-Hadi (The Guide).

Spiritual Tools and Practices to Enhance Your Routine

Tasbih (Prayer Beads): The misbaha is a Muslim prayer instrument composed of 99 beads; it's also occasionally referred to as a "tasbih" or "tasbeeh." Muslims frequently use them to record Dhikr prayers, which are said in remembrance of Allah's (SWT) benevolence.

Journaling Supplies: Use a notebook to document reflections on a name and its impact on your life.

Art Supplies: Create visual reminders (e.g., calligraphy of a name) to deepen your connection.

Intangible Practices

Mindfulness Meditation: Sit quietly, breathe deeply, and focus on a name of Allah (SWT), allowing its meaning to permeate your thoughts.

Gratitude Practice: Pair a name with daily gratitude. For example, thank Allah (SWT) for His provision while reflecting on Ar-Razzaq (The Sustainer).

Acts of Service: Embody the qualities of a name in your actions. Reflect Al-Karim (The Generous) by giving to others.

You can develop a greater comprehension of Allah's (SWT) qualities and how they apply to your life by making His name the main focus. Every name presents a chance to deepen your relationship with Him, turning everyday events into occasions for worship and introspection.

Chapter Eight

Utilising the Names of Allah (SWT) for Personal and Professional Goals

Setting and Achieving Goals with Divine Guidance

Islamic Sunnah calls for goal-setting, planning, and strategy development to ensure that objectives are met, and the Quran and the teachings of Prophet Muhammad (PBUH) support this. Therefore, planning must be at the core of their lives in all of a Muslim's moral, political, social, and economic endeavours.

Nothing that Allah (SWT) made is arbitrary or coincidental. He tells us that Everything that He created is measured and designed. Just like Allah (SWT) intended, accurate and exact. The Most High declares:

> "Indeed everything that we have created is according to a measure." (Quran 54:49)

Allah (SWT), the Creator of the earth and the skies, as well as of you and me, accomplished all of this via careful planning, accurate measurement, and design. He ordered everything to be done precisely, with a plan, in a methodical manner. Islam was founded on this planet only in accordance with a plan; it didn't come together with the rest of the world. The ultimate Prophet of Allah (SWT) arrived in accordance with Allah's (SWT) plan.

Making plans and establishing goals are essential components of leading a meaningful life. If we don't focus on larger goals, floating aimlessly through the days is simple. Without a route map, we frequently find ourselves overwhelmed and disoriented. We experience more than simply success when we match our plans with Allah (SWT); we also experience joy, fulfilment, and divine calm. Have you ever been unclear about your next goals? You're not alone. Because we neglect to present our plans to the One in control of the cosmos, many of us wander aimlessly.

Allah (SWT) has a divine purpose for every individual. It gives us confidence that His plans are not only good but also full of promise and hope. With this knowledge, we may make plans and set goals with confidence. It's about matching our goals with Allah's (SWT) grand plan, not just what we want. Allah's (SWT) intentions are greater than our comprehension and anticipation. Even though we may have our own plans and timeframes, we frequently end up in better places than we could have ever dreamed of when we submit to His divine plan and timeline.

Allah (SWT) has a limitless view, but our limited minds can only see so far. Because Allah (SWT) loves and desires the best for us, we have faith in His plans. When planning with Him, we give ourselves up to Allah (SWT)'s wisdom, direction, and rewards. This calls for humility and faith, understanding that even though we can make plans, His will ultimately win.

The Quran teaches us to plan and be strategic in our dealings. This is demonstrated in various ways, including the prophetic accounts, the natural rule of Allah (SWT), and the acclaim given to those with vision and foresight.

Prophet Yusuf (AS): His ability to interpret the king's dream and devise a 14-year economic strategy to save Egypt from famine (Surah Yusuf, 12:47-49) highlights planning for the long term and managing resources wisely.

Prophet Muhammad (PBUH): The Hijrah (migration) from Makkah to Medina was a meticulously planned endeavour, including choosing an alternate route, securing guides, and strategically timing the departure.

Role of Guidance and Success in Goal Setting

Setting goals can be a very effective way to achieve success. Well-defined and unambiguous goals foster motivation, focus, and a feeling of purpose. They help us focus our efforts on particular goals by providing a roadmap for resource allocation and decision-making. In our quest for self-actualisation, this helps us avoid wasting time on things, people, or locations that no longer benefit us.

By providing us with a feeling of direction, goals help us become more resilient and persistent. They make the objective more attainable by breaking down difficult activities into smaller, more doable steps. Setting and achieving goals also encourages ongoing learning and adaptation, which advances our long-term success and fosters personal development.

All things considered, goal-setting is a complex psychological phenomenon that satisfies basic human wants. When the reward system in the brain is engaged, it gives us a feeling of direction and purpose and enables us to experience a sense of accomplishment. The process demonstrates the intricate connection between human behaviour, motivation, and cognition, regardless of whether we're working towards an objective for personal fulfilment or outside rewards.

In a frequently unpredictable world, goals give us a sense of control. They offer a road map for overcoming obstacles and lessen fears of the future or the unknown. The goal-setting process taps into self-determination theory, a psychological concept based on the notion that independence, skill, and connection are basic human wants. Goal setting meets these needs by enabling us to establish our own goals, showcasing our abilities as we strive towards them, and cultivating relationships with like-minded individuals.

The human urge for direction and purpose is connected to the psychology of goal setting. Goals, which offer a framework for organising activities, provide a straightforward route to the intended results. Psychologically, this process uses mental functions like organising, making choices, and solving issues, which trigger the brain's reward circuits every time a milestone is completed. Our goal-directed conduct is reinforced largely by dopamine, a neurotransmitter linked to pleasure and reward.

A number of Allah's (SWT) beautiful names relate to guiding and achieving one's aims with success. For example, Al-Hadi, The Guide, reminds us of Allah (SWT) guiding His creation toward the right path. Every time we need clarification, either in life or when setting goals, supplication to Al-Hadi may lighten our way.

Similarly, Ar-Rashid emphasises Allah's (SWT) wisdom to guide us toward what is best for us. This is further complemented by the name An-Nur, The Light, as Allah (SWT) gives spiritual light to guide and help us distinguish the right direction when circumstances feel uncertain or overwhelming.

Names such as Al-Fattah (The Opener, The Judge) hold great appeal in the quest for success. This name signifies Allah (SWT) as the opener of doors of opportunity, the resolver of challenges, and clarifies the way forward. Similarly, Al-Karim (The Generous, The Benevolent) reflects the boundless generosity of Allah (SWT), where He provides resources and opportunities leading to success.

Al-Muqaddim, The Expediter, reflects Allah's (SWT) powers in advancing our efforts, ensuring that our actions bear fruit at the right time. This name instils trust in Allah's (SWT) plan for us as we continue striving toward our goals.

Equally important are names that remind us of Allah's (SWT) wisdom and might, crucial for achieving successful in our endeavours. Al-Hakim (The All-Wise) reminds us that Allah (SWT) grants wisdom to whom He wills, enabling them to plan and implement wisely. Alongside this is Al-Aziz (The Almighty) who reassures us of the strength required to overcome obstacles.

These qualities allow us to hold onto the fact that success can be achieved when we put our trust in Allah's (SWT) wisdom and power. In addition, Ash-Shafi attributes to Allah (SWT) the quality of being The Healer, who gives renewed health and motivation to pursue long-term objectives after we experience any failures.

Invoking these names during prayer and reflection creates an attachment of the heart with Allah (SWT) in guidance and strength for the journey. Remembering that success is ultimately from Allah (SWT) brings purpose, trust, and determination in pursuing our goals with the attachment to His divine guidance.

Strategies for Aligning Personal and Professional Goals with These Divine Attributes

Aligning personal and professional goals with the divine attributes of Allah (SWT) involves using these attributes as a guide to cultivate ethical, meaningful, and spiritually grounded pursuits in life. Here are strategies to achieve this alignment:

- **Commit to Justice and Fairness (Al-Adl)**

Even if justice turns against us, we Muslims should always stand up for justice as an exercise of principle, whether it's for Muslims or non-Muslims.

> *Allah (SWT) stated: "O you who believe, be persistently standing firm in justice as witnesses for Allah, even if it be against yourselves or parents and relatives. Whether one is rich or poor, Allah is more worthy of both. Follow not your desires, lest you not be just. If you distort your testimony or refuse to give it, then Allah is aware of what you do." (Quran 4:135)*

One of the fundamental principles of Islamic teachings is justice. The Islamic faith invariably includes whatever is just. We should never subjugate others because of our animosity toward them or their transgressions. Hatred is a terrible spiritual sickness that frequently results in acts of injustice directed at individuals rather than evil in general. Being fair and just has enormous rewards. On the Day of Judgement, those who uphold justice in all of their affairs will be granted a unique, elevated position.

Justice is a cornerstone of ethical living. In your personal life, treat everyone with fairness, avoid favouritism and bias, and advocate for equity in your relationships. In your career, ensure that your decisions, policies, and practices reflect integrity and fairness, fostering an environment where all are treated with respect and impartiality.

- **Cultivate Self-Sufficiency and Generosity (Al-Ghani)**

Islam emphasises the importance of self-sufficiency, urging people to take care of their own needs via their own efforts and to abstain from begging and idleness. Instead of complaining about our poverty, we must develop self-sufficiency by maximising our abilities. Despite obstacles and hard work, we should aim to generate a legal income to build a better future for ourselves.

The development of contentment is another facet of self-sufficiency. It implies living within our means and being content with the resources and means at our disposal. Our inflows and outflows ought to be balanced. We will benefit a lot if we can accomplish this. Our everyday issues will be fixed, and life will be simpler as a result of this blessing.

> *Abu Sa'id al-Khudri reported: The Messenger of Allah, peace and blessings be upon him, said, "Whoever would be independent, Allah Almighty will make him independent. Whoever would abstain from asking people, Allah Almighty will make him abstinent. Whoever is content with sufficiency, Allah Almighty will suffice him." (Sunan al-Nasai)*

Put your trust in Allah (SWT). As Muslims, we should have a strong faith in Allah (SWT). We should firmly believe that Allah (SWT) is the one who bestows gifts upon us, regardless of how meagre our resources may be. He causes the moon and sun to shine.

He creates a tree from a seed and extracts gold from between rocks. He is the one who extracts the pearl from the oyster. In a nutshell, Allah (SWT) has all authority and power. Thus, dependence on Allah (SWT) is the primary prerequisite for self-sufficiency.

It's more constructive to actively look for solutions to our difficulties rather than letting anxieties and concerns dominate us. We should endeavour to conquer or lessen the difficulties we face by utilising a variety of methods and techniques.

We should seek advice from a sincere, religious individual if we're unable to solve the problem on our own or if we're having trouble thinking rationally. According to the noble Quran, Sayyidunā Yūsuf (AS) used his knowledge, intelligence, and self-sufficiency to plan a feasible solution instead of succumbing to anxiety during the seven years of drought.

We are systematically encouraged to lead highly individualistic lives by the economic, social, and cultural systems in our environment.

According to popular culture, the goal of life is to pursue wealth and possessions with little regard for other people. Even while it's crucial to take care of oneself to a certain degree, the Holy Quran and the customs of the Holy Prophet (PBUH) teach us to constantly put others before ourselves. Islam is based on a generous mentality that inspires us to share our wealth, time, and mercy.

Being generous doesn't have to be complicated. Giving someone money may be as easy as that, but it could also include giving them time, energy, and attention. It may be a compliment, a handwritten message of gratitude, a smile, or a nice word. It could be cooking for someone, checking in on someone who is ill, encouraging them, or just listening.

Strive for self-reliance while remembering the importance of generosity. Personally, work to develop your skills and appreciate the blessings in your life. Professionally, share your resources and knowledge with others, supporting the growth and development of your community and workplace.

- **Show Gratitude and Appreciation (Al-Shakur)**

Islam places a strong emphasis on appreciation and thankfulness. Allah (SWT) will undoubtedly multiply the bounties of those who recognise and are thankful for them. In contrast, ingratitude has dire repercussions, as Allah (SWT) has said:

> *"And [remember] when your Lord proclaimed, 'If you are grateful, I will surely increase you [in favour]; but if you deny, indeed, My punishment is severe.'" (Quran 14:7)*

"Alhamdulillah," which translates to "all praise is for Allah (SWT)," opens the first chapter of the Quran. In our daily lives, the phrase "Alhamdulillah" means "gratitude." As a result, Muslims frequently say

"Alhamdulillah" in response to enquiries about how they are doing. In a same vein, Islam encourages people to express gratitude for everything during the day, including waking up, eating, drinking water, and more. In this sense, thankfulness for Allah (SWT) becomes the focal point of one's entire existence.

Similarly, someone who is appreciative of others will be liked and valued, while someone who lacks thankfulness and gratitude will be shunned and avoided. Every individual ought to live with a sense of appreciation and thankfulness for whatever comes their way.

Comparing what one receives with what others gain when granted something is wrong. A servant who receives favours from Allah (SWT) is required to express gratitude for them. Increasing acts of prayer and making use of the blessings in a way that pleases Allah (SWT) are two ways to express gratitude. In the same vein, good deeds should be returned with kindness rather than misbehaviour or harm. We truly show our thankfulness to Allah (SWT), the ultimate provider of all goodness, when we express appreciation to others.

Gratitude fosters positivity and strengthens relationships. Personally, regularly reflect on your blessings and express thanks to those who support you. In the workplace, acknowledge the efforts and contributions of colleagues, celebrating successes together to build morale and a sense of community.

By integrating these divine attributes into your goals and actions, you can create a balanced life that is both spiritually fulfilling and aligned with your highest purpose.

Motivating and Inspiring Action

A psychological trait and process known as motivation guides a person to take action toward a desired outcome. It can be thought of as a motivating factor that pushes or supports a course of action toward a goal. A person must first understand his or her purpose or aim to be motivated, while someone who lacks these things may experience motivation temporarily but not sustain it over time.

Motivation arises from a combination of conscious and unconscious elements, including the degree of need or want, the incentive or reward, the importance of the objective, and the individual's expectations. This is why Allah (SWT) says in the Quran that He desires people to be inspired constantly.

> *"And I have not created the jinn and mankind except that they should obey Me." (Quran 51:56)*

The sayings of Prophet Muhammad (PBUH) also inspire people to do certain things and avoid others. This guidance encourages people to avoid being avaricious and pursuing materialistic goals.

> *The Prophet (PBUH) stated: "Be in the life as if you were a stranger or a traveller on a path." (Bukhari)*

The Prophet's (PBUH) companions were extremely driven individuals. They were so driven that they were prepared to give up their money, time, families, and lives in order to follow Islam. Hazrat Abu Bakar (RA) gave up everything and left his home empty when the Prophet begged for alms. Abdur Rahman (RA) stepped up and gave nearly all of his gold while Medina was experiencing drought. Because of their profound faith in Allah (SWT), their strong dedication to the mission, and their strong conviction in the reward in the hereafter, the companions were highly driven.

Islam inspires people both within and externally. When someone is motivated by external stimuli, this is referred to as extrinsic motivation.

> *Allah (SWT) says in the Quran, "...and spend (in charity) from what we have provided from them secretly and publicly and prevent evil with good..." (Quran 13:22)*

The verse exhorts people to demonstrate their generosity in public since doing so will inspire others to do the same.

Stimuli that originate internally are referred to as intrinsic motivation. It has to do with a person's spirituality. A person must be internally motivated since Allah (SWT) the Exalted may not provide him with the reward here on Earth; instead, he must wait and exercise patience.

> *Allah (SWT) says in the Quran, "O you, who have believed, obey Allah and obey the Messenger..." (Quran 4:49)*

The individual is inherently inspired by this verse to follow specific instructions to obey Allah (SWT) and the Prophet (PBUH).

A person can only be motivated for a brief period of time by all material possessions. If someone needs to be inspired all the time, they should have a strong, unwavering faith in Allah (SWT), a strong belief in the rewards and punishments of the hereafter, and a strong dedication to the cause.

Names That Inspire Motivation, Ambition, and Perseverance

Contemplating such names can give us spiritual strength and resolve to face any hurdle and work towards perfection. Similarly, names related to inspiration and ambition, such as Al-Fattah (The Opener), remind us that Allah (SWT) opens the gates to benefit and success for those who work with honest commitment. This, in return, will make us hopeful and put in more effort.

Similarly, Al-Muqtadir reinforces the notion that Allah (SWT) provides us with the means and strength to reach success by encouraging us to aim high and go all the way to Him for support. Further, Al-Wahhab is a strong reminder of Allah's (SWT) giving, instilling hope that our efforts bring blessings beyond what could have been expected. Furthermore, Al-Alim (The All-Knowing) assures us that Allah (SWT) recognises our intentions and efforts, motivating us to work harder with confidence in His justice and wisdom.

Another quintessential characteristic that is developed through the names of Allah (SWT) is perseverance. As-Sabur (The Patient), imparts that patience indeed is a virtue in adversity. Contemplation of this name compels us to graciously and steadfastly bear adversities. Al-Qadir (The Omnipotent) reassures us that Allah's (SWT) control over all things enables us to persevere when the odds seem insurmountable. Al-Hakim (The Wise) reminds us that each trial has a purpose, encouraging us to trust Allah's (SWT) wisdom. Likewise, Ar-Razzaq comforts and empowers us since it confirms that Allah (SWT) sustains and provides for those who are patient and work hard.

By contemplating these names of Allah (SWT), we derive the spiritual strength that inspires our ambition and fastens it to its ultimate objectives. Each of these names can change our way of thinking and meet life's challenges with faith unshaken and undaunted.

Evaluating Progress and Reflecting on Achievements

The result of effort, hard work, and dedication is success. Celebrating success, whether it be a career victory, academic achievement, or personal milestone, is a crucial habit that raises our self-esteem and promotes ongoing development.

Amid our hectic lives, pausing to consider our accomplishments offers a priceless chance to value our path, recognise our development, and lay the groundwork for future endeavours. Daily reflection and progress reviews are essential for both professional and personal growth. It encourages learning from mistakes, goal alignment, and self-awareness.

Celebrating accomplishments increases motivation, and efficiency is increased through constant improvement and challenge adaptation. It keeps the long-term goal in mind while encouraging accountability, lowering stress, and fostering self-improvement behaviours. It's crucial to reflect on and evaluate your daily progress to improve your productivity and personal development.

Being thankful for everything we have is one of the most beautiful teachings Islam teaches us. Although we naturally consider things like our family, our food, and our health, we frequently overlook the fact that being Muslim is the greatest gift Allah (SWT) has given us. Consider this: You were selected to be a member of the Ummah out of billions of souls. Isn't that a great honour?

Indeed, religion has its share of difficulties because, let's face it, Shaytan is ruthless, and this life is extremely difficult. As a result, you may occasionally believe that Islam is a burden (Astaghfirullah) or that your faults make you unworthy of Allah's (SWT) consideration. But you shouldn't allow these doubtful moments to pull you away from what Allah (SWT) has given you, and the best way to accomplish that is to begin reflecting on the blessings He has given you.

Using Names Related to Reflection and Evaluation to Assess Progress

Using the names of Allah (SWT) for reflection and evaluation can provide a spiritual and mindful approach to assessing personal or professional progress. Here are some of Allah's (SWT) names that are particularly relevant to reflection, self-evaluation, and growth:

Al-Baseer (The All-Seeing): Reflect on how Allah (SWT) sees all things clearly and perfectly.

- **Self-reflection:** Am I being honest with myself about my intentions and actions?

- **Progress evaluation:** Are my actions aligned with the goals I've set? Are they pleasing to Allah (SWT)?

Al-Raqeeb (The All-Watchful): Allah (SWT) is always aware of what we do.

- **Self-reflection:** How conscious am I of Allah's (SWT) watchfulness over my actions and progress?

- **Progress evaluation:** Have I stayed consistent in my efforts, knowing that Allah (SWT) observes my work and struggles?

Al-Hasib (The Reckoner): Allah (SWT) will take account of everything.

- **Self-reflection:** Am I holding myself accountable daily for my deeds and goals?

- **Progress evaluation:** Am I tracking my growth systematically and honestly, as I would be accountable to Allah (SWT)?

By incorporating these names into your daily routine through journaling, prayer, and deliberate introspection, you can deepen your relationship with Allah (SWT) and make sure that His boundless mercy and wisdom direct your actions. In addition to assisting you in evaluating your progress, this approach fosters accountability, attention, and thankfulness, paving the way for ongoing spiritual and personal development.

Chapter Nine

Teaching and Sharing the Names of Allah (SWT) with Others

Educating Family and Friends

Teaching and sharing the names of Allah (SWT) with family and friends is a beautiful way to spread knowledge and deepen your faith. By explaining the meanings and significance of Allah's (SWT) names, we help others understand His attributes and how they can bring peace and guidance into their lives.

This practice encourages reflection on His mercy, power, and wisdom. Sharing this knowledge can also inspire others to develop a closer relationship with Allah (SWT), fostering a sense of community and spiritual growth. Also, educating those around us contributes to a stronger, more connected faith family.

Introducing the Names of Allah (SWT) to Children

Raising a Muslim child in this day and age can make it difficult to instil the fundamentals of Islamic education. However, if you begin teaching your children the names of Allah (SWT), it will not be a challenge. Teaching kids the fundamentals first creates a fascination that establishes a strong bond with Islamic ideas, which goes beyond simple education. What effect does teaching your kids the names of Allah (SWT) have on their early interest in Islamic education?

Applying Divine Qualities to Everyday Situations

Parents can teach the names of Allah (SWT) in meaningful ways by applying them to everyday interactions. Whether it's by thanking Allah (SWT) for the nourishment He provides as a family or by recognising His mercy when soothing a sobbing child. This integration turns your daily activities into instructive experiences.

Tawheed's True Nature Revealed

Tawheed, or the unity of Allah (SWT), can be understood through the names of Allah (SWT). Your children will start to understand the concept of Allah's (SWT) distinct and unrivalled features if you use straightforward stories and conversations about the holy attributes. Their path to deepening their religion is likewise firmly established by this early comprehension.

Telling Tales

Storytelling has always been an effective technique for captivating a child's imagination. By introducing the holy names of Allah (SWT) through captivating stories, as a parent, you not only make learning fun but also help your children develop a sincere comprehension and admiration of Allah's (SWT) magnificent qualities. It's equally crucial for you to have a relationship with your child based on love and Islamic principles. Through storytelling, especially bedtime stories, you can build their faith in Allah (SWT) and make your relationship with them a treasured ritual.

Developing a Feeling of Wonder and Appreciation

As parents, the development of thankfulness in our children is one of the only things that makes us happy. Introducing them to Allah's

(SWT) 99 names fosters amazement and thankfulness. Through learning these names, children come to appreciate the innumerable favours they've received and are amazed by the magnitude of Allah's (SWT) characteristics. This natural admiration serves as a beacon for their spiritual path and lays the groundwork for their Islamic journey.

Enhancing Worship

Our children's relationship with worship is strengthened when they comprehend the names of Allah (SWT). They start to understand the meaning and core of each name, whether it's during Salah (prayer) or other devotional activities. Their perception of the divine qualities is enhanced by the regular association of His names in their acts of prayer, which influences their Islamic journey.

It might be challenging to provide our children with a learning environment that helps them comprehend Islamic teachings more deeply, but teaching them the essence and qualities of Allah (SWT) through the 99 names can be an excellent place to start. Along with learning the names and their meanings, your children will develop an early interest in Islamic education. It turns education into a meaningful adventure, establishing the groundwork for a lifetime of love and faith-based knowledge.

Incorporating the Names into Family Activities and Discussions

Incorporating the names of Allah (SWT) into family activities and discussions can help create a spiritually nurturing environment. Here are some ideas on how to do so:

Name-Based Activities

Learn and Reflect: Choose one or two names of Allah (SWT) to focus on each week. Discuss the meaning and significance of these names during family meals or before bedtime. For example, you could talk about Ar-Rahman (The Most Merciful) and share examples of mercy in everyday life.

Memory Games: Create a memory game using cards with the names of Allah (SWT) and their meanings. Children can match the name with its meaning or a real-life example.

Incorporate into Daily Life

Prayers and Gratitude: Encourage family members to invoke the names of Allah (SWT) during prayer or while expressing gratitude. For example, when feeling thankful for something, use phrases like *Alhamdulillah* (Praise be to Allah (SWT)) or Ash-Shakur (The Most Appreciative).

Blessings on Meals: Before meals, remind everyone to say Bismillah (In the name of Allah (SWT)) and express gratitude. During meals, you can remind your family about Allah's (SWT) blessings and discuss how food is a gift from Him.

Incorporate Names into Conversations

Praise and Remembrance: Throughout the day, encourage family members to say phrases like SubhanAllah (Glory be to Allah (SWT)), Allahu Akbar (Allah (SWT) is the Greatest), and La ilaha illallah (There is no Allah (SWT) but Allah (SWT)). You can make this a habit during family walks, car rides, or even during chores.

Gratitude Discussions: When discussing achievements or blessings in life, link them to the names of Allah (SWT). For example, when someone excels at something, mention Al-Alim (The All-Knowing) and reflect on how Allah (SWT) has given knowledge and ability.

By weaving the names of Allah (SWT) into family routines and conversations, you foster a sense of spiritual mindfulness and encourage your family to live with an awareness of Allah (SWT) in their daily lives.

Creating Workshops and Learning Opportunities

Creating workshops and learning opportunities about the names of Allah (SWT) can be a powerful way to deepen understanding of Islamic teachings and help individuals connect with the divine attributes of Allah (SWT) in a practical and meaningful way. Below are some ideas for developing educational content and workshops:

Workshop Structure

Introduction to the Names of Allah (SWT):

- Objective: Introduce the concept of the Asma ul Husna (the 99 Names of Allah (SWT)) and explain their significance.

- Format: A short lecture or presentation explaining what the names are, their importance in Islam, and how they reflect Allah's attributes (such as mercy, power, knowledge, etc.).

- Activity: Share examples of the names in the Quran and their relevance in daily life.

Deep Dive into Select Names:

- Objective: Focus on a few key names (e.g., Al-Rahman, Al-Malik, Al-Alim) to explore their meanings and implications.

- Format: Break down each name, its linguistic roots, its attributes, and how to incorporate these names into one's daily prayers, actions, and thoughts.

- Activity: Group discussions on how these names can be reflected in family life, work, community, and worship.

Online Learning Modules

Objective: Provide a digital platform (e.g., website, app, or video course) for learning about the names of Allah (SWT).

- Interactive Lessons: Include interactive quizzes, flashcards, and activities where participants can test their knowledge.

- Visual and Audio Aids: Use audio recordings to teach pronunciation of the names, along with visual presentations showing the meaning of each name.

- Reflection Videos: Create short, inspiring videos in which scholars or speakers reflect on how each name can guide personal development and spirituality.

Collaborative Learning Events

Community-Based Workshops: Create community-focused workshops where attendees can participate in group activities, share their experiences, and learn together.

Name of the Month Sessions: Organise sessions where the community comes together to learn about and reflect on a specific name of Allah (SWT). This could be held in mosques, community centres, or online.

Feedback and Continuous Learning

Surveys and Feedback: Collect feedback from participants at the end of each workshop to understand what was most helpful and what could be improved. This will help in tailoring future content and activities.

Advanced Workshops: Offer advanced workshops for those who want to delve deeper into the understanding and application of Allah's (SWT) names in their personal and communal lives.

By developing well-structured content and offering interactive learning opportunities, these workshops can foster a deeper spiritual connection to the names of Allah (SWT) and help participants understand how to reflect those divine attributes in their everyday lives.

Chapter Ten

Reflecting on the Impact of Using Divine Names

Assessing Personal Growth and Transformation

The idea of personal development in Islam is firmly based on the knowledge that serving and worshipping Allah (SWT) is our ultimate goal in life. This encompasses how we behave in all facets of our lives and goes beyond the conventional ideas of worshipping at a mosque or just praying.

> The Quran reminds us, *"And I did not create the jinn and mankind except to worship me."* (Quran, 51:56)

Accordingly, from an Islamic standpoint, personal development entails more than merely attaining financial success or personal fulfilment. To help humanity and fulfil our obligation to Allah (SWT), we must strive to become the best versions of ourselves.

For millions of people worldwide, Islam is a beacon of hope, providing a holistic framework that fosters individual and collective growth in various areas. Islamic principles, which have their roots in the teachings of Prophet Muhammad (PBUH) and divine direction from the Quran, offer Muslims practical avenues for ongoing spiritual, intellectual, moral, and social development.

Islamic teachings strongly emphasise self-improvement, urging followers to constantly examine their deeds, ask for forgiveness, and pursue excellence in them. Muslims engage in self-reflection through self-help activities, including goal-setting and forming constructive habits, as well as daily supplications (dua) and assistance from religious mentors. They are also stressed to cultivate patience and resilience in the face of adversity, as these traits support spiritual development and emotional health.

Incorporating the names of Allah (SWT) into personal or spiritual practice often powerfully affects one, fostering greater self-awareness and a deeper connection to higher principles. Revered across many traditions, divine names invoke a sense of reverence, focus, and inner change. Transformation through spiritual practice often occurs in quiet yet powerful ways, influencing both inner and external life. Regular reflection upon these changes keeps one aligned with one's purpose and aware of where one has been.

Reflecting on How Using the Names Has Influenced Personal Development

Meditating on, reciting, or invoking these names can have a transformative impact on personal development, fostering growth in faith, character, and daily life.

Enhancing Spiritual Awareness

Engaging with the Names of Allah (SWT) often deepens one's connection to the Creator. Each name serves as a reminder of Allah's (SWT) infinite attributes, encouraging self-reflection and alignment with divine qualities:

Al-Wakeel (The Trustee): Reciting this name instils trust in Allah's (SWT) plan, helping to manage stress and relinquish control over uncertain situations. This awareness brings a sense of inner peace and purpose as one learns to rely on Allah (SWT) while striving for self-improvement.

Cultivating Emotional Resilience

There are obstacles and hardships in life. As Muslims, we know that this world will put us to the test.

> *Allah (SWT) says in the Quran: "We will certainly test you with a touch of fear and famine and loss of property, lives, and crops. Give good news to the steadfast." (Quran 2:155)*

Although hardship is unavoidable, how we handle it shows who we are. We cannot only endure life's hardships but also get stronger as a result of cultivating patience and resilience.

Using the Names of Allah (SWT) in dhikr (remembrance) or prayer helps manage emotions and overcome challenges. For example, invoking As-Salam (The Source of Peace) calms the heart during moments of anxiety, promoting mental clarity and calmness. Reflecting on Al-Qahhar (The Subduer) helps individuals recognise that difficulties are part of Allah's (SWT) greater wisdom, encouraging patience, surrender, and acceptance. Regularly engaging in these practices nurtures emotional resilience and a balanced perspective on life's ups and downs.

Strengthening Character and Conduct

A fundamental need of the Muslim faith is decent morals and manners, which requires careful consideration and work.

Prophet Muhammad (PBUH) said: "The best amongst you are the best in character and manners." (Al-Bukhari)

But developing our character is by no means a simple undertaking. It takes a lot of self-control, observation, and instruction to completely change the way we think and behave. Islam is centred on morality, politeness, and good character. The goal of all Islamic sciences is to improve people's behaviour, both internally and externally, as well as their interactions with Allah (SWT) and other people.

Indeed, manners and character are two sides of the same coin, two facets of the same ethical reality. Manners (Al-Adab) are the external behaviours that people display, whereas character (Al-Akhlaq) is the attributes that exist within the heart. Put another way, good character naturally manifests in good manners.

Therefore, we must learn how to cultivate a pure heart and the appropriate social conduct that goes along with it. All of the lessons we acquire in Islam are designed to improve us as individuals, as Allah's (SWT) servants, and as fellow humans. When we comprehend this, we'll be able to handle complex issues and contemporary difficulties without becoming misguided or filled with hatred.

Each of Allah's (SWT) names serve as a model for personal behaviour, guiding us to embody divine qualities in our actions:

Al-Adl (The Just) encourages fairness and integrity in dealings with others, while Al-Karim (The Generous) inspires acts of kindness and charity, cultivating a generous spirit. This conscious effort to emulate Allah's (SWT) attributes fosters moral and ethical growth, enriching relationships and social interactions.

The inner and outer aspects of existence are transformed when one uses the Names of Allah (SWT) in spiritual practice. It cultivates a mind based on divine insight, a heart anchored in faith, and deeds that honour Allah's (SWT) exquisite attributes. This path of self-discovery demonstrates the significant influence of incorporating spirituality into everyday life.

Seeking Knowledge and Wisdom

The quest for knowledge is one of Islam's core precepts. According to the Prophet Muhammad (PBUH), every Muslim is required to seek knowledge. This focus on knowledge encompasses more than just academic learning; it also includes developing one's wisdom, self-awareness, and self-improvement.

"Knowledge is power," as the saying goes. The Quran has long emphasised the importance of pursuing knowledge in Islam, starting with the first revelation to our beloved Prophet Muhammad (PBUH). Regardless of one's ethnic background, age, nationality, social standing, or other characteristics, every Muslim is obliged to pursue knowledge. As liberating members of the Ummah, we all have an equal right to education and the pursuit of knowledge to better ourselves.

There are several passages in the Quran and hadiths that discuss the need to pursue knowledge in addition to the well-known surah on the subject, Surah al-'Alaq, where the entire chapter emphasises how urgent it is for every Muslims to read or learn:

> *"Allah (SWT) will raise up, by many degrees, those of you who believe and those who have been given knowledge: He is fully aware of what you do." (Quran 58:11)*

Allah (SWT), the Glorious, promises that those who acquire knowledge will rise in rank. It's clear that the learned are at a far greater level than the uneducated.

"He has subjected all that is in the heavens and the earth for your benefit as a gift from Him. There truly are signs in this for those who reflect." (Quran 45:13)

As you can see, Allah (SWT) states in numerous places throughout the Quran that those who think and contemplate, particularly while using their intellect, will discover the signs that the uninformed miss. Continue your education and explore the world's wonders; you'll find Allah's (SWT) magnificent signs among them. Pursuing knowledge will broaden your perspective, making you wise, smarter and more mature.

What Does Knowledge Exactly Mean in Islam?

Fundamentally, the term "knowledge" denotes comprehension and awareness of a certain topic or area. In Islam, pursuing knowledge is more than just acquiring facts; it involves a deep effort to understand and absorb the teachings, tenets, and precepts of Islam.

Exploring the huge reservoir of Islamic teachings, which cover a wide range of topics like theology, legal theory, ethics, history, and spirituality, is the essence of seeking knowledge in Islam. It entails not just learning information by heart but also comprehending the ramifications and deeper meanings of these lessons.

Islam emphasises the importance of knowledge in all facets of life and views it as a sacred and fundamental notion. Islamic scholars emphasise the value of pursuing knowledge to achieve self-realisation, complete earthly tasks, and eventually enter Paradise. They also view knowledge as an offering from Allah (SWT) that allows people to improve both intellectually and spiritually by connecting them to heaven.

Islamic teachings hold that knowledge is a multifaceted and universal entity rather than being divided into religious and non-religious spheres. Islam places a strong emphasis on the pursuit of knowledge with Prophet Muhammad (PBUH), highlighting that it's the duty of every Muslim to do so to avoid Hell and become enlightened spiritually.

Knowledge as a Prerequisite to True Worship

According to Al-Imam Al-Ghazali in his book *Minhaj Ul-'Abideen*, we must first know Allah (SWT) in order to perform acts of devotion and avoid mistakes. Without understanding His divine names, attributes, and essence, how can we worship Him? He went on to say that we must understand our religious duties and obligations, know what is required of us to fulfil them and recognise the factors that compel us to refrain from actions that are forbidden.

The internal acts of worship that centre on things of the heart are then subject to the same command of knowledge. These include interior stations like sincerity, patience, repentance, and Tawakkul. Then, we must also be aware of and refrain from the antithesis of admirable qualities, such as arrogance, ostentation, and excessive anger. Our inner and exterior states of devotion, which are attained via knowledge, are the points that have been described. Then, knowledge and performance are inextricably linked (Amal).

A virtue is the pursuit of knowledge via appropriate means. For the seeker, it offers numerous benefits. Put another way, one can achieve its benefits through a serious effort to learn rather than by becoming a highly competent scholar.

> *The Prophet (SWT) stated in a hadith: "Whoever takes a path in search of knowledge, Allah will cause him to walk in one of the paths to Paradise. Indeed the angels will lower their wings in great pleasure with the one who seeks knowledge." (Sunan Abu Dawud)*

Learning about Islam is unquestionably important for Muslims' spiritual and personal development and is a basic obligation for all believers. To improve their life, give back to society, and strengthen their relationship with Allah (SWT), Muslims are urged to pursue knowledge in a variety of subjects. The quest for knowledge is a continuous journey that changes people, builds communities, and has an impact on the world. This emphasises how important it is to seek out Islamic knowledge, awakening, and the truth.

Sharing Testimonies and Success Stories

Documenting and sharing personal testimonies and success stories can be a powerful way to inspire and connect with others. If you focus on how the Names of Allah (SWT) have impacted lives, you can create meaningful content that uplifts and strengthens faith. Here's a framework to help you effectively share these stories:

Documenting and Sharing Personal Success Stories and Testimonies

To begin, it's essential to gather authentic and heartfelt stories. Reach out to friends, family, or community members who are willing to share their experiences. These could be moments when they invoked a specific name of Allah (SWT) and saw a transformation in their lives.

For example, someone might share how calling upon Ar-Razzaq (The Provider) brought unexpected sustenance during financial hardship or how reflecting on As-Salam (The Source of Peace) helped them find tranquillity amidst the chaos. If you're comfortable, include your own personal stories, which can add a unique and relatable touch. To respect privacy, offer contributors the option to share anonymously.

When presenting these stories, structure them in a way that draws the reader in. Begin with an introduction that outlines the challenge or situation the individual faced. Follow this by describing how invoking a particular name of Allah (SWT) became a turning point, emphasising the connection between the attribute and the circumstances. Conclude with the outcome and the impact, highlighting how the experience deepened their faith or brought about a resolution. By focusing on the transformation, you showcase the power of trusting in Allah's (SWT) names and attributes.

Ultimately, these stories can serve as a powerful tool for inspiring others. They remind us that Allah's (SWT) names are not just abstract concepts but living attributes that can bring about change in our daily lives. Through these testimonies, readers can find encouragement to call upon Allah (SWT) with conviction, seeking His guidance and blessings in their own journeys.

Chapter Eleven

Continuing Your Journey with the Names of Allah (SWT)

Setting Long-Term Spiritual and Personal Goals

One of the best ways to strengthen your faith and maintain your relationship with Allah (SWT) is by setting personal goals. It provides you with direction, meaning, and a goal to strive for on your spiritual path.

Start by identifying what matters most in your relationship with Allah (SWT). Setting meaningful goals that actually matter is possible when you are aware of your priorities.

The first step to a transforming spiritual path is to centre your aspirations on what Allah (SWT) wills. Real spiritual change takes time to manifest. It calls for dedication and a readiness to keep looking for Allah's (SWT) knowledge and direction.

Over time, long-term objectives can help you stay on course and grow in your faith.

Developing Long-term Plans for Incorporating the Names into Daily Life

Incorporating the names of Allah (SWT) into daily life is a meaningful way to deepen one's spiritual connection and align actions with divine attributes. The process can begin with understanding and memorising the Asma ul Husna (Beautiful Names of Allah (SWT)).

A practical approach is to learn and reflect on a few names each month, starting with those frequently used in prayers, such as Ar-Rahman (The Most Merciful) and Ar-Rahim (The Most Compassionate). Studying their meanings and linking them to Quranic verses or hadith can enrich understanding. Over time, committing all 99 names to memory and contemplating their significance can become a long-term goal.

Integrating the names into daily worship is another step. This can be as simple as including specific names in duas tailored to one's needs, such as invoking Al-Ghaffar (The Forgiving) when seeking forgiveness or Ar-Razzaq (The Provider) when asking for sustenance. Developing a habit of dhikr (remembrance) by reciting the names after salah or during quiet moments can create a steady rhythm of spiritual mindfulness. Personalised duas that reflect the meanings of Allah's (SWT) names can further enhance one's connection to Him.

Embodying the values of Allah's (SWT) names in daily actions is a powerful way to live by these divine attributes. For instance, one can practice mercy in interactions to reflect Ar-Rahman, show fairness in decisions to emulate Al-Adl (The Just) or cultivate patience in difficult times inspired by As-Sabur (The Patient). Regular self-checks can help assess whether personal actions align with these values, encouraging continuous growth and alignment with Islamic principles.

Creating a spiritual environment is another way to keep Allah's (SWT) names present in daily life. Displaying them in one's home as reminders or using digital tools like apps and flashcards can help reinforce familiarity. Engaging family members by discussing one name each week and exploring its relevance can foster a shared spiritual journey. Journaling about how Allah's (SWT) attributes manifest in everyday experiences can deepen personal reflection and gratitude.

Teaching and sharing the names of Allah (SWT) with others is a way to spread this spiritual awareness. Sharing reflections with friends or family and discussing how they can implement these attributes in their lives creates a ripple effect of inspiration. Participating in or initiating study circles centred on Allah's (SWT) names can foster a sense of community. For those inclined, writing or presenting insights about the names can further encourage others to connect with their Creator in meaningful ways.

The names of Allah (SWT) can also be integrated into specific areas of life. At work, invoking Al-Fattah (The Opener) for guidance in new opportunities and calling upon Al-Amin (The Trustworthy) in dealings can bring barakah (blessing) to professional endeavours. In relationships, embodying forgiveness inspired by Al-Ghaffar or showing gratitude in the spirit of Ash-Shakur (The Appreciative) can strengthen bonds. During challenges, turning to Al-Qawiyy (The Strong) for resilience or Ar-Raheem for comfort can provide solace and motivation.

Finally, connecting Allah's (SWT) names to life events can make those moments more spiritually meaningful. Naming children or initiatives after His attributes, such as Rahma (Mercy) or Nur (Light), can be a lifelong reminder of His presence. Reflecting on Allah's (SWT) role during significant events, such as acknowledging Al-Hafiz (The Preserver) for protection during hardships, can reinforce trust in His divine wisdom.

By incorporating these practices into daily life, one can create a holistic and enduring connection with the names of Allah (SWT). This intentional approach allows His attributes to inspire and guide every aspect of one's existence, fostering spiritual growth and harmony.

Maintaining Consistency and Commitment

Behaving or performing similarly is referred to as consistency, as is performing particular acts on a regular basis. A key habit for success is consistency. If you don't regularly make wise decisions and conduct appropriately, you probably won't accomplish anything. Even if our actions are small, they should be consistent; the fact that you consistently carry them out for Allah's (SWT) sake demonstrates your love and loyalty to your Creator.

Strategies for Staying Committed to Using the Names Regularly

Consistently invoking the names of Allah (SWT) can deepen faith and enrich your spiritual life. Here are some strategies to help you stay committed:

Understand Their Meaning: Take time to study the 99 Names of Allah (SWT), their meanings and their significance. Reflect on how each name manifests in your life. This understanding makes the act of invocation more heartfelt and purposeful.

Set a Routine: Integrate the Names of Allah (SWT) into your daily schedule. For instance, recite specific names during morning and evening supplications or after each prayer. Start small, focusing on a few names each day and gradually expand.

Use Visual Reminders: Place calligraphy or posters of Allah's (SWT) names in visible areas at home or work. This serves as a constant reminder to engage with them.

Incorporate in Duas: Begin or conclude your prayers by calling on Allah (SWT) through His Names, particularly those relevant to your needs (e.g., Ar-Rahman for mercy, Al-Fattah for ease).

Stay Consistent: Use apps, journals, or trackers to monitor your progress. Celebrate small milestones to maintain motivation.

Reflect on Benefits: Regularly remind yourself of the peace and spiritual closeness you experience through this practice, reinforcing your commitment to it.

Exploring Further Study and Practice

The Names of Allah (SWT) hold immense spiritual depth, offering endless opportunities for reflection and growth. To deepen your connection with Allah and strengthen your practice, consider the following approaches:

Encouraging Continued Exploration

Reflective Contemplation: Spend time meditating on the meanings of specific names, considering how they manifest in your life and the world around you. For instance, reflect on Al-Wadud (The Most Loving) by observing acts of love and kindness in creation.

Memorisation and Application: Gradually memorise the Names of Allah (SWT) and incorporate them into your daily duas. Applying their meanings to your supplications strengthens your relationship with Allah (SWT).

Teaching and Sharing: Share what you learn with family or friends. Discussing and teaching the Names of Allah (SWT) can solidify your understanding and inspire others.

Personal Projects: Start a journal where you write reflections on each name or create artwork or poetry inspired by their meanings.

Immerse yourself in the beauty of Allah's (SWT) Names, letting them guide your worship and enrich your faith.

Chapter Twelve

Conclusion

In conclusion, our exploration of Allah's (SWT) 99 Beautiful Names, the Asma ul Husna, reveals their profound impact on both our spiritual growth and daily lives. These names provide a roadmap for leading a purposeful, balanced life, offering infinite wisdom, compassion, and strength. As we contemplate each name, we are inspired to cultivate virtues such as resilience, humility, love, justice, patience, and forgiveness, all of which shape our actions, decisions, and inner peace.

Each name of Allah (SWT) holds a unique significance that helps us navigate life's challenges. For example, Al-Rahman (The Most Merciful) teaches us compassion, encouraging forgiveness and understanding in our relationships, Al-Adl (The Just) promotes fairness, while Al-Sabur (The Patient) reminds us to trust in Allah's (SWT) timing and embrace patience. Al-Hakim (The Wise) inspires us to seek knowledge and act thoughtfully, guiding us to approach life with clarity and calm.

These divine names also enrich our relationships. Al-Wadud (The Loving) fosters kindness and care, while Al-Ghaffar (The Forgiving) encourages us to release resentment and nurture harmony. Professionally, the Asma ul Husna directs us toward integrity, honesty, and ethical conduct, emphasising the importance of prioritising others' well-being over material gain. Names like Al-Mu'min (The Giver of Security) and Al-Razzaq (The Provider) encourage us to create safe spaces and rely on Allah (SWT) for sustenance, motivating us to act with dedication and responsibility.

As we integrate these qualities into our lives, we align ourselves with a higher purpose and find strength, clarity, and peace. Life's challenges become opportunities for growth, and the Asma ul Husna guides us toward continuous self-improvement, leading to spiritual fulfilment. May these names inspire and guide us, bringing us closer to Allah (SWT) and enriching every aspect of our lives.

Find Out More

Website: www.barakahinbusiness.com

Socials: @barakahinbusiness

If you enjoyed this book, kindly leave a review to help expand our reach so others may benefit also.

www.ingramcontent.com/pod-product-compliance
Lightning Source LLC
Chambersburg PA
CBHW071212070526
44584CB00019B/3008